221
Plants
Encyclopaedia

MANOJ PUBLICATIONS

221 Plants Encyclopaedia

Publisher:

MANOJ PUBLICATIONS

761, Main Road, Burari, Delhi-110084
Ph.   : 91-11-27611116, 27611349
Fax   : 91-11-27611546, Mob. : 09868112194
E-mail   : info@manojpublications.com
For online shopping visit our website :
www.manojpublications.com

Showroom :

1583-84, Dariba Kalan, Chandni Chowk, Delhi-110006
Ph.   : 91-11-23262174, 23268216
Mob.   : 09818753569

ISBN : 978-81-310-2297-9

CONTENTS

Introduction

The world of plants is very fascinating. We see a variety of plants around us. Human beings, other animals and plants are the living organisms that exist on Earth. Plants are adapted to nearly every environment on Earth. Some grow in frigid, ice-bound polar regions and others grow in hot, dry deserts. All plants need water, but some plants cannot live unless they are submerged in either freshwater or salt water.

Plants range in size from microscopic water ferns to giant sequoia trees that are sometimes more than 100 metres in height. Most have root-like structures that hold them in the ground or onto some other objects like a rock or another plant.

So, it can be said that plants:

- are found on land and in water-bodies.
- need water to grow healthy.
- are the sole source of food for all living organisms.

What are plants?

Plants are the only organisms able to sustain themselves by producing their own food. In turn, they provide food for animals and humans, through the food chain. Plants are characterised by the following features:

- Their unlimited growth throughout their lifespan (their embryonic tissues or meristems remain active throughout)
- Their photosynthesis method of preparing food
- Their cells contain cellulose in their walls (this makes plant cells more or less rigid)
- They lack the organs of locomotion, sensory and nervous system.

Difference between plants and animals

Plants have one common characteristic that makes them different from animals. Plants, such as trees, flowers, fruits and vegetables, produce chlorophyll, a substance that allows them to convert solar energy into nutrition, or food. On the other hand, animals as well as humans obtain their nutrition either by consuming plants or other animals. However, there are some plants that are not able to use sunlight and soil to produce their own source of energy. For example, moulds are parasites that obtain their energy directly from the plant or animal they live on—their host. Furthermore, plants such as moulds do not reproduce through seeds; they reproduce by creating spores.

Plants have taken a relatively short time in the history of our planet to evolve into a diverse group. The great plant communities have, in turn, helped the evolution of insects, fungi and vertebrates. Over 270,000 species of plants have been identified and classified so far, but scientists believe that there are millions more waiting to be discovered.

Classification of plants

There are different kinds of plants around us. They vary in sizes, shapes, colours, smell, places of growth, etc.

Category I

On the basis of their sizes and types of stems, plants can be classified into the following categories:

Trees

Some plants are very tall, and have hard and thick brown stems. These stems have branches in the upper part, much above the ground. Such plants are called trees.

Herbs

The plants with green and tender stems are called herbs. They are usually short and may not have many branches.

Shrubs

Some plants have the stems branching out near the base. The stem is hard but not very thick. Such plants are called shrubs.

Climbers

The plants with weak stems that take support on neighbouring structures and climb up are called climbers.

Creepers

The plants with weak stems that cannot stand upright and spread on the ground are called creepers.

Catergory II

Other than the above classification, plants can also be categorised as flowering plants and non-flowering plants. They are divided into groups based on the traits they have in common. Scientists change the way plants are classified from time to time, when they discover new types of plants or learn new things about plants.

The two main groups are:

Vascular plants

The plants that use stems and veins to transport food and water are vascular plants.

Vascular plants can be divided into smaller groups, one of which is a seed plant. This group includes flowering and non-flowering plants.

Flowering plants include monocots (one-seed leaf) and dicots (two-seed leaves). All green plants that have flowers are called flowering plants. Scientists have grouped these according to the number of seed leaves found in each plant.

Dicot seeds usually have two cotyledons that are attached to and enclose the embryonic plant. A monocot has a single thin cotyledon that functions to transfer food from the endosperm to the embryo.

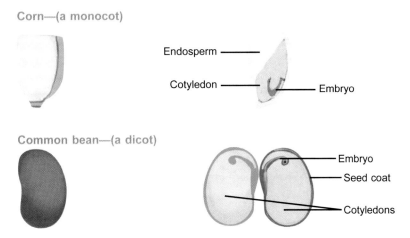

Corn—(a monocot)

Endosperm ———

Cotyledon ———

Embryo

Common bean—(a dicot)

Embryo

Seed coat

Cotyledons

The plants without flowers are called **non-flowering plants** or gymnosperms. While they do produce seeds, the seeds are not enclosed in a flower (and eventually a fruit). Non-flowering plants are very common, and include evergreens (conifers), cycads and ginkgo. Popular types of conifers include fir and pine trees.

The main difference between flowering and non-flowering plants is their method of reproduction. Flowering plants rely on pollination for reproduction, whereas non-flowering plants rely on dispersion to continue their life-cycle.

Non-vascular plants

The plants with no roots, stems or leaves are non-vascular plants. Example: moss.

Structure of plants

There is an infinite variety of plants. The difference among the various plants can be identified on the basis of: their root systems, their shoot systems and their arrangement of leaves.

But all plants share certain common features. Plants, in spite of their diversity, have the same architecture. Plants grow at the tips throughout their life. All parts of plants have an outer covering.

All plants transport water and nutrients upwards from the roots. All plants conduct food produced in the leaves to the other parts.

Parts of plants

A plant generally has a **root system** and a **shoot system**. There are some plants that do not have distinct root systems or shoot systems.

Shoot system

Root system

Parts of plant

Root system

Roots fix a plant in the soil, absorb water and nutrients from the soil, and store sugars and starch for future use.

All plants have roots, but all roots are not the same. Pull out a bean plant and some tufts of grass. Compare their roots. The root of the bean plant is long and tapering. It has small branches of roots and root hair. They are called **tap roots**.

Fibrous root

A taproot system has one central root from which smaller, lateral roots branch out. Roses, carrots and apple trees are the examples of the plants with taproot systems.

Grasses have no main root or taproot. The roots of grass are bunched together and spread out horizontally. They are called **fibrous roots**.

Tap root

In a nutshell, a root can be:

- long as in a bean plant (tap root system).
- bunched at the base and grow laterally as in grasses (fibrous root system).
- swollen as in a carrot (modified root system).
- growing from the branch to the ground as in a banyan tree (aerial root system).

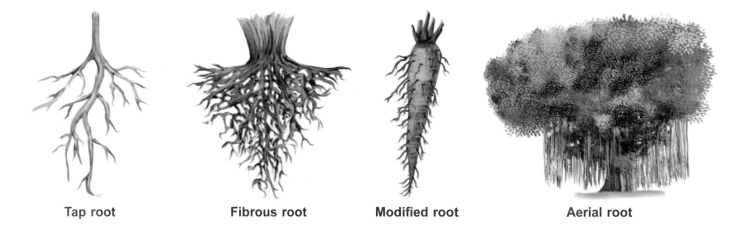

| Tap root | Fibrous root | Modified root | Aerial root |

Functions of roots

Roots are important to plants because of the following functions:

- Roots fix plants to the ground.
- Roots absorb water and nutrients from the soil.
- Roots fix the soil and provide additional support (in some plants).
- Some plants store food in their roots. These types of roots can be eaten.

Shoot system

The shoot of a plant can be considered as the portion that is generally above the ground, lies above the seeds.

The shoot system of a plant consists of both the stem and the leaves.

The stem provides the framework to position the leaves properly. Flowers, fruits and seeds are formed on the shoots.

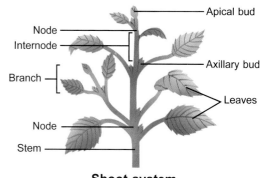

Shoot system

Stem

The stem is the link between the roots and the leaves and flowers. It generally holds the plant upright. The stem of a tree is called the **trunk**. The trunk is the strongest part of a tree, covered with bark which protects the inner parts of the tree. Some plants have weak stems.

Stems have the following parts to perform various functions:

1. **Nodes** are the places where the leaves are formed.
2. **Internodes** are the portions (the intervals on the stem between the nodes) between the nodes.
3. **Buds** are small projections from which shoots, leaves or flowers develop.
4. **Axil** is the angle between a leaf and the stem to which it is attached.
5. **Terminal bud** is the growing portion of the plant at the apex of the shoot. By the continued development of this bud and its adjacent tissues, the stem increases in height.

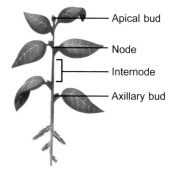

Parts of stem

Functions of the stem

- It provides support and a framework to the plant.
- It helps leaves to face the sun.
- It houses the twin transporting channels.
- Some plants store food in their stems, that can be eaten.

The twin transporting channels in plants

The vascular plants have an efficient system to conduct water and nutrients from roots and carbohydrates (food) prepared in the leaves to all parts of the plant through two separate tubes or channels.

The two channels have specialised cells and run parallel to each other. The fluids flowing through the two channels never get mixed. Water and nutrients (in solution) are used by the leaf to prepare food and the sugar molecules manufactured in the leaves are used for growth.

The modified stem—Is it root or stem?

This grows underground. But this is actually a **stem**.

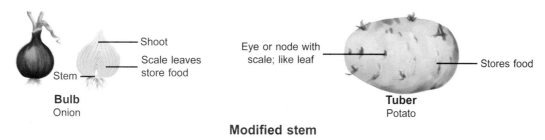

Modified stem

Cactus—Is it stem or leaf?

Cactus is green. But it is not a leaf. It is a modified stem.

- The stem of cactus stores food.
- It stores water for long periods.
- It synthesises food.
- It has spines to reduce transpiration. Spines are actually leaves.

The cactus stem shows the modification required for survival in hot and dry places.

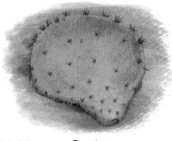

Cactus

Leaf

A large plant or a big tree has hundreds of leaves. A leaf grows on the stem or branch of a plant. Leaves are often the most abundant part of a plant. We often identify plants by the shape and colour of their leaves. Leaves come in a wide variety of shapes, sizes, and colours.

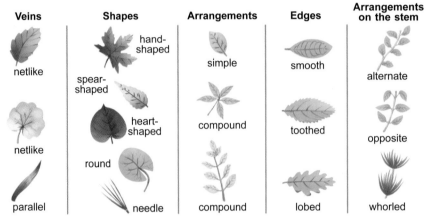

Types of leaves

Parts of a leaf

Blade: The blade, or lamina, is the broad, flat part of the leaf. Photosynthesis occurs in the blade, that has many green food-making cells.

Petiole: The petiole is the stem-like part of the leaf that joins the blade to the stem.

Midrib: The midrib is the main, central vein of the leaf.

Stipules: The stipules are two small flaps that grow at the base of the petiole of some plants.

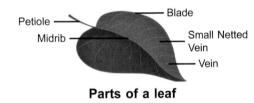

Parts of a leaf

Veins: The veins are on the underside of the leaves. The arrangement of the vein in all the leaves is not the same. Veins may be parallel or a network.

Functions of leaves

- They make food with the energy of sunlight.
- Leaves perform **photosynthesis**, resulting in the production of sugar.
- They provide air to the plant.
- They regulate the moisture (**transpiration**) in a plant.

Transpiration

Transpiration involves the movement of water into the roots along xylem vessels and finally through the leaf cells to be evaporated. This evaporation or transpiration takes place through the stomata. Transpiration acts like a suction pump that draws water from the roots against gravity up the xylem tubes to the leaves. This pressure is enough to transport water to the top of the tallest tree.

Flowers

Flowers produce seeds that form new plants. Plants use flowers to reproduce (make more of themselves). The job of a flower is to produce a fruit, which contains seeds. Flowers are used by humans to add beauty to outdoor and indoor areas, and some flowers can also be eaten.

Parts of a flower

The important parts of a flower are:

Sepal: It is a modified leaf that forms the outer whorl of a flower. It is mostly green in colour and protects the flower bud.

Petal: The second whorl of modified leaves, usually brightly coloured to attract pollinators to visit the flower.

Stamens: One or two whorls of highly modified leaves form the stamens. Stamen is the male reproductive organ of the plant that produces pollen. It consists of a filament and an anther.

Stigma: It is at the top of the style and is coated with a sticky substance to trap the pollen grains that fall on it.

Style: It is a tube-like structure in the centre of a flower that supports the stigma.

Pistil: It is composed of one or more separate or fused carpels (leaves). The terminal parts of leaves form the stigma that receives the pollen during pollination.

Whorl of a flower

A whorl is a circular arrangement of flower parts around a point on an axis.

How plants make food

Leaves are called the food factory of life on Earth. Each part of a plant is an amazing demonstration of an efficient organisation. The leaf has the most efficient organisation.

Leaves are the sunlight-capturing part of the plant. With the help of this sunlight, leaves produce food. This whole process of producing food by leaves with the help of sunlight is called **photosynthesis.**

Photosynthesis

Photosynthesis is a complex chemical process that takes place in the leaves of plants to manufacture carbohydrates for their food.

The raw materials of photosynthesis are: carbon dioxide from the air (taken in through leaves) and water (usually from soil) taken in through the roots. **Sunlight** is the energy source and **chlorophyll** or green pigment provides the energy required to carry out photosynthesis.

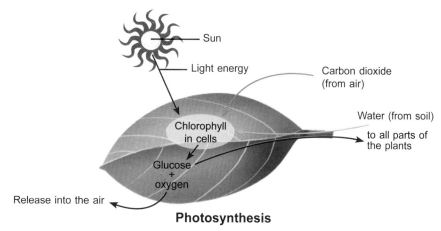

Photosynthesis

Chlorophyll

Most plants have green leaves. Leaves look green because they contain a colouring pigment called chlorophyll. Plants use chlorophyll to capture the light energy of the sun and store that energy as sugar. Chlorophyll is found in the **chloroplasts** of leaves.

The green chlorophyll molecule bears a striking resemblance to haemoglobin (the red pigment in blood that carries oxygen). Plants use chlorophyll to derive energy from sunlight through a complex series of chemical reactions (photosynthesis).

Chemical process of photosynthesis

Water is first broken down to oxygen (which is released to the atmosphere) and hydrogen by photosynthesis (breaking down by light). Hydrogen then reduces carbon dioxide to simple sugars containing hydrogen, carbon dioxide and oxygen.

Photosynthesis is a complex process taking place in many stages, but the reaction can be summed up by the simple equation:

$$6CO_2 + 6H_2O \xrightarrow{\text{(Light + chlorophyll)}} C_6H_{12}O_6 + 6O_2$$

Carbon dioxide + Water   Glucose + Oxygen

Why are plants important?

Plants play a critical role in the ecosystem. During photosynthesis, plants convert carbon dioxide into oxygen, which is vital for humans and other animals to stay alive. Also, the moisture that evaporates from the leaves of plants accounts for 10 per cent of the water in the atmosphere. Plants are also an important source of nutrients for humans and animals. Even if the animal itself does not eat plants, something it eats will eat plants.

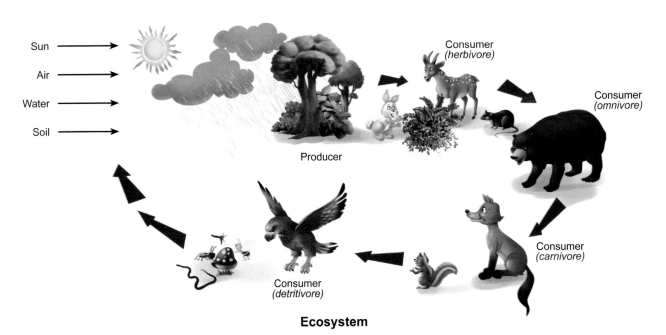

Ecosystem

Plants are an important source of income worldwide. People earn income by growing and selling materials that come from plants. Many other careers involve working with plants as well. Farmers, landscapers, and forest rangers must know a great deal about plants, so must chefs, textile designers, home and boat builders, botanists and numerous other professionals.

1. Abelia

- **Common name** : Glossy Abelia
- **Scientific name** : *Abelia grandiflora*
- **Family** : Caprifoliaceae
- **Native land** : Eastern Asia (Japan west to the Himalayas) and Southern North America (Mexico)

Abelia is a perennial deciduous shrub. It was first raised in 1886 at the Rovelli nursery at Pallanza (now Verbania), on Lake Maggiore in Italy. This is a rounded, semi-evergreen shrub. It grows up to 6 feet tall. It has ovate, glossy, dark green leaves, which turn purplish-bronze in autumn. The flowers have fragrance. The greatest bloom is usually observed in the late summer, with fruit and seed production starting in summer and continuing until autumn. It is used as an ornamental plant in specimen plantings in gardens.

2. Acalypha

- **Common name** : Jacob's Coat
- **Scientific name** : *Acalypha wilkesiana*
- **Family** : Euphorbiaceae
- **Native land** : Fiji and neighbouring South Pacific Islands

It is an evergreen, often suckering, tropical shrub, annual outdoor houseplant. It can grow up to 10-15 feet tall in frost-free areas. The leaves are coppery green with red splashes of colour. This gives them a mottled appearance. The leaves are large and broad with teeth around the edge. The plant blooms periodically throughout the year, although it is somewhat hidden. It can be grown in a warm greenhouse or as a specimen or hedging plant (especially in warm areas). Its ointment is used to treat fungal skin diseases.

3. Acer

- **Common name** : Silver Maple, Red Maple
- **Scientific name** : *Acer saccharinum/Acer rubrum*
- **Family** : Sapindacea
- **Native land** : Eastern North America (White Maple)/ Eastern and Central North America (Red Maple)

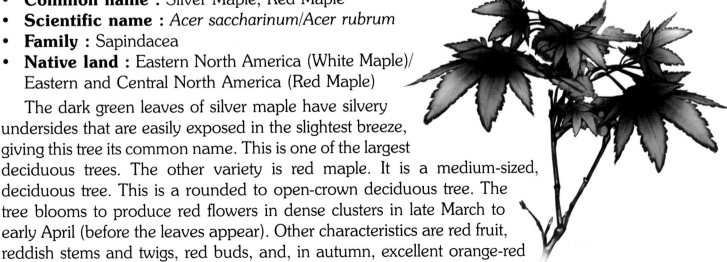

The dark green leaves of silver maple have silvery undersides that are easily exposed in the slightest breeze, giving this tree its common name. This is one of the largest deciduous trees. The other variety is red maple. It is a medium-sized, deciduous tree. This is a rounded to open-crown deciduous tree. The tree blooms to produce red flowers in dense clusters in late March to early April (before the leaves appear). Other characteristics are red fruit, reddish stems and twigs, red buds, and, in autumn, excellent orange-red foliage colour.

4. Achillea

- **Common name** : Yarrow
- **Scientific name** : *Achillea millefolium*
- **Family** : Asteraceae
- **Native land** : Europe, Western Asia, North America

The name 'Achillea' comes from Achilles, the hero of the Trojan War in Greek mythology, who used the plant medicinally to stop bleeding and to heal the wounds of his soldiers. It is a rhizomatous, spreading, upright to mat-forming perennial. The plant grows up to 2 feet tall. It produces deeply-dissected, fern-like, aromatic, medium green foliage and tiny, long-lasting, white flowers. The flowers are produced in flat corymbs in early to late summer. The plant is used for cottage gardens, wild gardens, meadows, prairies and naturalised areas.

5. Aconite

- **Common name** : Monkshood
- **Scientific name** : *Aconitum napellus*
- **Family** : Ranunculaceae
- **Native land** : Western and Central Europe

The name 'monkshood' is derived from the shape of the flowers, which look like blue helmets. It is a herbaceous perennial plant. The leaves are rounded, palmately divided into five to seven deeply lobed segments. They have hooded flowers produced on stalks well above the toothed foliage, with colourful sepals providing the shape and colour. Aconite was traditionally used in western medicine as an anaesthetic. It has been replaced by safer drugs. It is still used in very small amounts in traditional Chinese medicine for Yang deficiency, or energy depletion.

6. Aeonium

- **Common name** : Saucer Plant
- **Scientific name** : *Aeonium undulatum*
- **Family** : Crassulaceae
- **Native land** : Northern Africa and surrounding areas

The plant is an evergreen perennial or small, semi-woody shrub with fleshy, tidy, rosette leaves. Leaves grow in a variety of colours and patterns, from light green to variegate with deep purple. Aeonium plants grow up to 3 feet tall. Flowers appear in spring to summer. The plants are grown in temperate greenhouses, in borders, or as house plants. One characteristic of these plants is the very sticky stem of the inflorescence. Small stalks with flowers continue to appear for several months.

7. African Violet

- **Common name** : African Violet
- **Scientific name** : *Saintpaulia*
- **Family** : Violaceae
- **Native land** : East central Africa

It was first discovered in 1892 in East Central Africa by Baron Walter von Saint Paul-Illaire. It is a herbaceous perennial flowering plant, usually grown indoors. It is popular due to its ability to thrive in low light conditions and bloom throughout the year. It is available in a wide range of colours and types, and can be easily cultivated through root cuttings or seeds. It has fleshy downy leaves and five-petalled flowers, usually with a distinct eye. African violets are best grown in the dappled shade of deciduous trees that allows full winter and spring sunshine.

8. Agapetes

- **Common name** : Himalayan Lantern
- **Scientific name** : *Agapetes serpens*
- **Family** : Ericaceae
- **Native land** : The Himalayas

The plant is an evergreen perennial. It is an odd member of the blueberry family. The plant has long, arching stems adorned with scarlet, jewel-like blooms. The fascinating patterns of this plant make it a very artistic addition to the garden. The branches themselves are beautiful, with their artistic rows of small, closely-spaced leaves often tinged with red. The delightful blooms appear from about February through June, and occasionally other times of the year. It is mostly grown in climates from cool temperate to sub-tropical. It can be propagated from cuttings.

9. Agastache

- **Common name** : Mexican Hyssop
- **Scientific name** : *Agastache mexicana*
- **Family** : Labiatae
- **Native land** : Southern North America

It belongs to the family of mint and is a perennial and self-fertile plant. Typical of the mint family, the stems are square and they can grow up to 4 inches tall. There are about 30 species of agastache. The plant grows well in full sunny conditions but should be protected from any extreme conditions such as high winds. It is used in Mexican folk medicine to treat anxiety, insomnia and pain. The younger leaves possess slight lemon-like odour. These young leaves can be used in tea or as a herb in salads or cooked dishes.

10. Agave

- **Common name :** Century Plant
- **Scientific name :** *Agave attenuata*
- **Family :** Asparagaceae
- **Native land :** The plateaus/mountains of Central Mexico

Century plant is a rosette forming evergreen herbaceous perennial succulent. It is popular for its attractive leaves and its huge drooping flower stems. Spineless, fleshy, ovate, light grey to pale yellowish-green evergreen leaves form a large symmetrical rosette. Each rosette will flower only once, usually when the plant reaches about 10 years old. Flowers are followed by seed pods. Additional common names for this plant include lion's tail, swan's neck and foxtail. Agaves are wonderful, low maintenance plants for gardens, needing little water or care.

11. Alcea

- **Common name :** Hollyhock
- **Scientific name :** *Alcea rosea*
- **Family :** Malvaceae
- **Native land :** Asia and Europe

The plant is variously described as a biennial (having a two-year life cycle), as an annual, or as a short-lived perennial. There are about 60 species of this flowering plant. They can grow up to 7 inches. It is an easy-to-grow plant, and is available in a variety of colours including some shade of white, pink, or purplish red. It blooms from July to September, and the seeds ripen from August to October. The plant also has nutritional properties. A nutritious starch is obtained from the root and a refreshing tea is made from the flower petals. Its leaves have a mild flavour. So, it can be added to salads.

12. Alder

- **Common name :** Seaside Alder
- **Scientific name :** *Alnus maritima*
- **Family :** Betulaceae
- **Native land :** The United States

The name 'Maritima' comes from Latin, meaning growing by the sea. It is a deciduous, multi-trunked, upright-rounded, fall-blooming perennial large shrub or small tree that typically grows to 20-30 feet tall. The greatest bloom is usually observed in the late summer, with fruit and seed production starting in summer and continuing until autumn. The leaves are not retained year-to-year. The seaside alder has a moderate lifespan relative to most other plant species and a moderate growth rate. At maturity, a typical seaside alder will reach up to 30 feet high. It is mainly used as a windbreak.

13. Alfalfa

- **Common name :** Alfalfa
- **Scientific name :** *Medicago sativa*
- **Family :** Papilionaceae
- **Native land :** Asia Minor and the Caucasus Mountains (warmer temperate climates)

It is a perennial flowering plant. The plant shows numerous small clover-like spikes of blue or violet flowers of upright growth. The plant grows to a height of up to 3 feet. Alfalfa has been used as a herbal medicine for over 1,500 years. The foliage is greatly relished by horses and cattle. Alfalfa leaves contain eight essential amino acids. It is a good source of many vitamins and minerals like calcium and magnesium.

14. Alliaria

- **Common name :** Garlic Mustard
- **Scientific name :** *Alliaria petiolata*
- **Family :** Brassicaceae
- **Native land :** Europe, including Britain, South to North Africa and East to West Asia and the Himalayas

It is a biennial flowering plant in the mustard family. The plant has delicate green leaves and snow-white flowers. The leaves are broadly heart-shaped, stalked, with numerous broad teeth. The fruits are black, cylindrical, and grooved. They ripen between mid-June and late September. Garlic mustard is used as a medicine to treat gangrene and ulcers. The leaves of garlic mustard are rich in vitamin C and A, and are used in sauces and salads. Additionally, garlic mustard can be planted for erosion control.

15. Amaranth

- **Common name :** Tampala
- **Scientific name :** *Amaranthus tricolor*
- **Family :** Amaranthaceae
- **Native land :** South Central Mexico

It is an annual or short-lived perennial plant. Amaranth now has worldwide distribution. The amaranth plant is a grain and greens crop plant. The plant develops long flowers, which can be upright or trailing depending on the variety. The flowers are used to produce the amaranth grain, while the leaves can be used as amaranth greens. Amaranth is excellent raw in salads, used as a steamed vegetable, and included in soups and stews. *Amaranthus tricolour* bears large leaves in brilliant shades of red, yellow, bronze and green on handsome plants reaching up to 6 feet high.

16. Ambrosia

- **Common name** : Western Ragweed
- **Scientific name** : *Ambrosia psilostachya*
- **Family** : Asteraceae
- **Native land** : North America, nearly all of the continental United States, and the Northern half of Mexico

It is a perennial herb. It grows like a slender, branching, straw-coloured stem to a maximum height near two metres, more often remaining under one metre tall. Leaves are lance-shaped to nearly oval, and they are divided into many narrow, pointed lobes. The stem and leaves are hairy. Western ragweed was used in teas for various medicinal purposes by several Amerindian tribes. This plant provides good grazing for wildlife and poor grazing for livestock.

17. Amelanchier

- **Common name** : Saskatoon, Juneberry
- **Scientific name** : *Amelanchier alnifolia*
- **Family** : Rosaceae
- **Native land** : North Western and North Central & North America

The city, Saskatoon (in Saskatchewan, Canada) is named after the berry. It is a perennial deciduous shrub. The ripe juneberry fruit is dark purple, with several tiny soft seeds. These berries serve as a food source for mammals and birds, and the dense growth provides shelter. The shrub has good nutrient levels throughout the year. It is browsed mostly in spring when it provides good forage for cattle, goats, sheep, and wild ungulates. The fruits are eaten fresh and are used while preparing puddings, pies, and muffins. The berries are also dried like raisins and currants.

18. American Lotus

- **Common name** : American Lotus, Yellow Lotus
- **Scientific name** : *Nelumbo lutea*
- **Family** : Nelumbonaceae
- **Native land** : Eastern North America

It is an herbaceous flowered aquatic perennial with large circular leaves. It is commonly found in lakes and swamps, as well as areas subject to flooding. Flowering begins in late spring and may continue into summer. This plant has a large tuber that is used as a food source. The seed of the plant is also edible. The seed of this plant is commonly known as 'alligator corn'. The seed receptacles are popular additions to dried flower arrangements.

19. Amsonia

- **Common name** : Willow Blue Star
- **Scientific name** : *Amsonia tabernaemontana*
- **Family** : Apocynaceae
- **Native land** : North America, East Asia and the Eastern Mediterranean

It is a perennial plant, first discovered in 1788. It is found in wooded areas and on riverbanks. It blooms in May and June. Each flower has five pale blue flower petals and blooms in clusters on two to three-foot stems. The upright stems with narrow leaves are attractive all summer and turn into beautiful butterscotch-yellow in autumn. The plants grow in full sun to light shade. Narrow, willow-shaped, dull green foliage may turn into an attractive yellow in autumn.

20. Anemone

- **Common name** : Wood Anemone
- **Scientific name** : *Anemone nemorosa*
- **Family** : Ranunculaceae
- **Native land** : Europe

It is one of the first spring flowers appearing in March and April. It is a perennial and spread by means of underground roots. The deeply-cut leaves and star-like flowers rise directly from it on separate unbranched stems. In sunshine, the flower is expanded wide, but at the approach of night, it closes and droops its graceful head so that the dew may not settle on it and injure it. The various parts of the plant were used medicinally by the ancient herbalists for headache, tertian ague (tertian malaria) and rheumatic gout.

21. Anise

- **Common name** : Anise, Star Anise
- **Scientific name** : *Illicuim verum*
- **Family** : Schisandraceae
- **Native land** : North-East Vietnam and South-West China

It is a medium-sized native evergreen tree. Star Anise is so named from the stellate form of its fruit. The star-shaped fruits are picked just before ripening and dried before use. It is often chewed in small quantities after each meal to promote digestion and sweeten the breath. The fruit is used in the East as a remedy for colic and rheumatism, and in China for seasoning dishes, especially sweets. It has come into use in the West as a less expensive substitute for anise in baking as well as in liquor production.

22. Apocynum

- **Common name :** Spreading Dogbane
- **Scientific name :** *Apocynum androsaemifolium*
- **Family :** Apocynaceae
- **Native land :** North America

It is a perennial herb. The bloom season starts from June and ends by August. The flowers are bell-shaped, pink to white with pink stripes on the inside. Each flower has five flaring lobes that curl back. The leaves are toothless, usually hairy underneath, sometimes have slightly wavy edges, and may be drooping. The fruit is a slender long pod that ripens from green to a dull red. It is used as an alterative in rheumatism, syphilis and scrofula. The plant is also helpful in dropsies due to heart-failure.

23. Apricot

- **Common name :** Apricot
- **Scientific name :** *Prunus armeniaca*
- **Family :** Rosaceae
- **Native land :** China, Armenia or Siberia

Apricot is a hardy, medium-sized deciduous tree. The fruits are often categorised as 'stone fruits' because of the stony seeds. The leaves are broad and roundish, with a pointed apex. The fruit ripens by the end of July to mid-August, according to variety. It is a drupe with a thin outer, downy skin enclosing the yellow flesh. Apricot oil closely resembles the oil of almonds and is frequently used in cosmetics. Apricots can be consumed in both fresh and dried forms. It is rich in dietary fibre, antioxidants, vitamins, and minerals.

24. Aquilegia

- **Common name :** Colorado Blue Columbine
- **Scientific name :** *Aquilegia caerulea*
- **Family :** Ranunculaceae
- **Native land :** Rocky Mountains from Montana south to New Mexico and west to Idaho and Arizona

It is a native perennial. It is the state flower of Colorado. The flower was first discovered in 1820 by botanist and mountaineer Edwin James. The flowering stems usually reach above the foliage and carry spurred, bell-shaped, often pendulous flowers in shades of blue and purple, as well as red, yellow, and white. The flowering period can vary among the species; some bloom through much of late spring and summer; others are short-flowering. It often attracts hummingbirds.

25. Arabis

- **Common name :** Georgia Rockcress
- **Scientific name :** *Arabis georgiana Harper*
- **Family :** Brassicaceae
- **Native land :** The US, Georgia

Georgia rockcress is a perennial herb with unbranched stems up to 3 feet tall. It generally grows on steep river bluffs with shallow soil on rock or with exposed rock outcroppings. The small white four-petalled flowers bloom in a loosely branched cluster at the top of the stem. The basal leaves are toothed and spoon-shaped, while those on the lower stems are narrow and strap-like. The plant prefers a sunny situation on dry to moderately moist soil for growth. Georgia rockcress plant is listed as an endangered species under the Endangered Species Act.

26. Araucaria

- **Common name :** Norfolk Island Pine
- **Scientific name :** *Araucaria heterophylla*
- **Family :** Araucariaceae
- **Native land :** Norfolk Island, 1,000 km off the east coast of Australia

It is an evergreen, coniferous tree. It looks like a pine with horizontal needle-like branches, but it is not part of the pine genus. It is one of the most familiar tree silhouettes in the world. The dark green leaves (needles) are awl-shaped, covering all sides of the branches, changing their shapes slightly in the upper branches as the tree ages. The bark is grey and rough. It is also popular as a Christmas tree, or as an exotic houseplant of ancient lineage that survives with little watering.

27. Arenaria

- **Common name :** Woods Sorrel
- **Scientific name :** *Oxalis arenaria*
- **Family :** Oxalidaceae
- **Native land :** South America

It is a perennial herb. Wood sorrel has adapted to grow in forest shade. It is a fragile rhizome with creeping characteristics. Its leaves have long stalks with three leaflets and flowers have five petals. The flowers appear in shades of white, yellow, lavender, or rose. The fruit is capsule-shaped. It blooms in spring and again in autumn. The flowers have some ornamental value. The flowers are preferred by insects, but the plant has poisonous effect on human beings. When ingested in large quantities, the leaves may cause trembling and cramps.

28. Armeria

- **Common name :** Thrift
- **Scientific name :** *Armeria maritima*
- **Family :** Plumbaginaceae
- **Native land :** Eurasia, North Africa, and the American Pacific coast

It is a perennial garden flower. There are about 80 species of this plant. Armeria got the name 'thrift' because of its ability to grow well even in harsh conditions. It is a popular garden flower. It is an ideal candidate for cottage gardens, and is also used as cut flower. These flowers can be used fresh or dried. The plant can grow in dry, sandy, saline conditions such as those at beaches and salt marshes. In some places, its leaves and roots are used as an anti-obesity agent.

29. Artichoke

- **Common name :** Artichoke
- **Scientific name :** *Cynara scolymus*
- **Family :** Asteraceae
- **Native land :** Mediterranean region

It is one of the popular winter season, edible flower buds. It is a perennial plant. The ideal growing conditions for artichoke are cool and moist summers and mild winters. It grows up to 1.5-2.0 metres in height, with arching, deeply lobed, silvery-green leaves. The bud is composed of compactly arranged triangular scales in a whorl fashion around a central 'choke'. Artichokes are low in calories and fat. It is a rich source of dietary fibre and anti-oxidants. Fresh artichoke is an excellent source of vitamins, folic acid and minerals like copper, calcium, potassium, iron, manganese and phosphorus.

30. Arugula

- **Common name :** Arugula, Salad Rocket
- **Scientific name :** *Eruca sativa*
- **Family :** Brassicaceae
- **Native land :** Mediterranean region, from Morocco and Portugal in the west to Syria, Lebanon and Turkey in the east

It is an edible annual plant, commonly known as salad rocket. It is one of the nutritious green leafy vegetables of Mediterranean origin. Its light green leaves appear identical to that of spinach in younger plants. Additionally, young, tender leaves feature sweet flavour, and less peppery taste in contrast to strong, spicy flavour in case of mature greens. In general, arugula grows to about 2-3 feet in height. It produces creamy-white edible flowers. Green leafy arugula is a very good source of vitamins and minerals.

31. Aruncus

- **Common name :** Goatsbeard
- **Scientific name :** *Aruncus dioicus*
- **Family :** Rosaceae
- **Native land :** Northern hemisphere in North America, Europe, and Asia

The word 'Aruncus' comes from the Greek word aryngos (goat's beard) and refers to the feathery plume of flowers. It is a herbaceous, perennial plant. It is found along the edges of forests and streams, and in moist woods and meadows. The spectacular display of goat's beard makes it a popular choice for gardeners, particularly those who like to garden with native flora. The plant can be started from seed, but takes a long time to grow and become established. It grows up to 6 feet. The seeds of this plant provide food for birds in autumn and winter.

32. Asclepias

- **Common name :** Common Milkweed, Pleurisy Root
- **Scientific name :** *Asclepias syriaca*
- **Family :** Apocynaceae
- **Native land :** Eastern half of the United States and Southern Great Plains

It is a native perennial plant. It grows best in rich sandy or gravelly loam soils. It contains a sticky white sap that is mildly poisonous. It is an important plant because many species of insects depend on it. This showy plant is frequently grown from seed in home gardens. Its brilliant flowers attract butterflies. The plant usually has a single stem and grows up to 6 feet in height. It has large, broadly oblong leaves, usually four to ten inches long. Its tough roots are chewed as a cure for pleurisy and other pulmonary ailments.

33. Asparagus

- **Common name :** Garden Asparagus
- **Scientific name :** *Asparagus officinalis*
- **Family :** Asparagaceae
- **Native land :** Eastern Mediterranean and Asia Minor areas

It is a spring vegetable, a flowering perennial. It is available from early September to March. An asparagus plant can grow up to 39–59 inches tall. It has stout stems with much-branched feathery foliage. The leaves are needle-like cladodes (modified stems) in the axils of scale leaves. The fruit is a small red berry which is poisonous to humans. Rich in vitamins B and C, calcium, and iron, asparagus is well known as a diuretic and laxative. It is useful to those who have a sedentary lifestyle and suffer from the symptoms of gravel. It has been found very beneficial in cases of dropsy.

34. Aspen

- **Common name :** Poplar, Quaking Aspen
- **Scientific name :** *Populus tremula*
- **Family :** Salicaceae
- **Native land :** Northern Hemisphere

Poplar is a slender deciduous tree that grows up to 30 metres tall. It displays a smooth, grey-green bark, random branching, rich green leaves that turn brilliant yellow during autumn. Poplar trees are either female or male. In spring, both male and female trees produce dense clusters of tiny flowers called catkins. They are distinguished by the shape of their leaves that are pointed at the tip. It is an important factor in maintaining the biodiversity of forest ecosystems. The bark of the tree is chiefly used in intermittent fevers. It has been employed as a diuretic in urinary infections.

35. Asplenium

- **Common name :** Hart's-tongue Fern
- **Scientific name :** *Asplenium scolopendrium*
- **Family :** Aspleniaceae
- **Native land :** Michigan and New York, Japan and Europe

It is an evergreen fern. It has an unusual, almost tropical appearance, with wide, leathery-green fronds that are strap-shaped. Plants form a low clump, best suited for rock gardens or for edging in a moist woodland garden. The plant attracts butterflies. It grows well in humus-rich, moist but well-drained soil. Bright midday sun can cause damage. People consume Hart's-tongue ferns to treat digestive disorders and urinary tract diseases.

36. Aster

- **Common name :** Aster Zigzag
- **Scientific name :** *Symphyotrichum prenanthoide*
- **Family :** Asteraceae
- **Native land :** Eastern North America and Eastern Canada

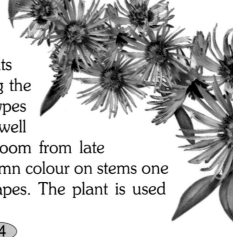

The plant is named after the curious twist in its leaves. It is a perennial flowering plant. It is among the last flowers of autumn. This plant grows in many types of habitats, including woody and marshy areas as well as roadsides. The beautiful blue-purple flowers bloom from late summer through early autumn providing great autumn colour on stems one to three feet tall. The leaves vary in sizes and shapes. The plant is used medicinally to treat fevers in babies.

37. Aubrieta

- **Common name :** False Rockcress
- **Scientific name :** *Aubrieta deltoidea*
- **Family :** Brassicaceae
- **Native land :** European mountains

This belongs to the cabbage family and is a perennial plant. But it is widely planted in rock gardens worldwide as an ornamental plant. It forms a low cushion of evergreen leaves, literally smothered by flowers for several weeks. It grows up to 6 to 8 inches tall. The flower colour ranges from mauve/lilac, mixed purple, red, to pink. There are about 12 species of this plant. The purple flowers are held in small bunches above unusual plump foliage. The plants look superb when grown on a dry stone wall where the plants can cascade down over the edges.

38. Avocado

- **Common name :** Avocado
- **Scientific name :** *Persea americana*
- **Family :** Lauraceae
- **Native land :** Mexico, Central America and South America

It is a multi-stemmed tropical evergreen tree. Avocado leaves are typically glossy, elliptic to ovate and dark green. Small greenish-yellow flowers bloom in panicles, followed by green-skinned, pear-shaped to rounded fruit. Each fruit has a very large central seed or pit surrounded by an edible fruity pulp. Mature fruits ripen off the tree, with the edible flesh turning yellow with a rich buttery consistency. Avocado is one of the very few fruits that is packed with 'good' mono-unsaturated fat. It is also very rich in fibres, vitamins and minerals.

39. Azalea

- **Common name :** Rosebay
- **Scientific name :** *Rhododendrons azalea*
- **Family :** Ericaceae
- **Native land :** South-Eastern Asia, North-Western Himalayas, Tibet and Western and Central China extending south and east to Malaysia and the Philippines

It is the national flower of Nepal. It is an evergreen, shrub-type plant with bell-shaped flowers. Evergreen azaleas are dense, usually shapely plants. Azalea bushes can grow mostly upward or spread outward, depending on the type. They range from less than 1 foot to more than 15 feet tall. Azaleas are among the most important of garden plants. They bloom in spring, their flowers often lasting several weeks. The flower and the fruit of the shrub are used to make popular fruit and flower wines.

40. Azolla

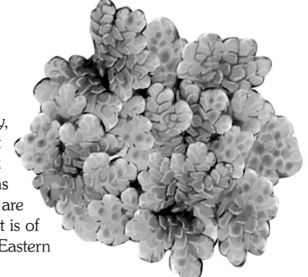

- **Common name** : Mosquito Fern
- **Scientific name** : *Azolla caroliniana*
- **Family** : Salviniaceae
- **Native land** : North, Central and South America

It is an annual floating fern and resembles algae. Normally, azolla is grown in paddy fields or shallow water bodies. It multiplies very rapidly. The plants can be dark green, dark red, or dark green with red margins. Thin, branched stems are covered by leaves. Small numbers of unbranched roots are also produced. It is a rich source of protein and vitamins. It is of commercial importance in cultivation in Southern and Eastern Asia as a bio-fertiliser.

41. Bachelor's Button

- **Common name** : Cornflower
- **Scientific name** : *Centaurea cyanus*
- **Family** : Asteraceae
- **Native land** : Europe, North America and parts of Australia

It is an annual flowering plant. The plant blooms from late spring to summer. It grows up to 3 feet tall. Most plants grow roughly 1 to 3 feet tall and have short, lance-shaped lyrate-pinnatifid leaves. The charming delicate flowers come in a variety of brilliant colours, and make excellent cut flowers. Each flower has overlapping bracts. The flowers attract butterflies. It is grown as an ornamental plant in gardens, where several cultivars have been selected with varying pastel colours, including pink and purple. A decoction of cornflower is effective in treating conjunctivitis, and as a wash for tired eyes.

42. Bacopa

- **Common name** : Water Hyssop/Brahmi
- **Scientific name** : *Bacopa monnieri*
- **Family** : Plantaginaceae
- **Native land** : Wetlands of Southern India, Australia, Europe, Africa, Asia, and North and South America

It is a perennial, creeping herb. The leaves of this plant are succulent, oblong and 4-6 millimetres thick. The leaves are oblanceolate and are arranged oppositely on the stem. It is a popular aquarium plant due to its ability to grow in water. The flowers are small and white, with four or five petals. In India, it is used as an Ayurvedic medicine for the treatment of a number of disorders, particularly those involving anxiety, intellect and poor memory.

43. Bamboo

- **Common name :** Common Bamboo
- **Scientific name :** *Bambusa vulgaris*
- **Family :** Poaceae
- **Native land :** East Asia, Eastern and Southern India and the Himalayas, Northern Australia, sub-Saharan Africa, Argentina and Chile

Bamboos are the flowering perennial evergreen plants. They are some of the fastest-growing plants in the world. Certain species of bamboo can grow up to 35 inches within a 24-hour period. There are about 1460 species of bamboo on the Earth. These species are found in diverse climates, from cold mountains to hot tropical regions. In China, it is used as a Chinese medicine for treating infections and healing. Bamboos are used to make furniture. Soft bamboo is used to make various food-products.

44. Bank Cress

- **Common name :** Land Cress
- **Scientific name :** *Barbarea verna*
- **Family :** Brassicaceae
- **Native land :** South-Western Europe and Florida

This is a biennial plant. The plant grows up to 1 feet tall. The basal leaves are dark green, shiny and deeply lobed with a tall yellow flower spike in spring. It can be grown almost all year round, with protection in colder months. The plant can be easily grown in ordinary soil with plenty of light or part shade. This plant self-seeds and supplies us with lots of greens over winter and early spring. The leaves of this plant are used in sandwiches and salads. They can be cooked like spinach, or used in soup and fish.

45. Barbarea

- **Common name :** Winter Rocket
- **Scientific name :** *Barbarea vulgaris*
- **Family :** Brassicaceae
- **Native land :** Eurasia, North America

They are small herbaceous biennial or perennial plants with dark green, deeply lobed leaves and yellow flowers with four petals. The stem is ribbed and hairless, branched at the base. The fruit is a pod of about 15-30 millimetres. It blooms from May to July, and the seeds ripen from June to August. The leaves are highly nutritious and a good source of vitamins and minerals. The leaves are used as an ointment for treating wounds.

46. Basil

- **Common name :** Basil/Tulsi
- **Scientific name :** *Ocimum basilicum*
- **Family :** Lamiaceae
- **Native land :** Africa and Asia (India, China, South-East Asia, and New Guinea)

It is an annual herb. In India, basil is believed to be imbued with divine essence. A number of varieties exist today, ranging from tiny-leafed Greek basil to robust 2-foot-high plants with large succulent leaves. Some varieties have deep purple leaves. While the flowers are typically small and whitish, some can be pink to brilliant magenta. The leaves can be dried for later use. Basil is extremely frost-sensitive. It is mostly associated with Mediterranean cooking but also very prevalent in Asian food. Basil has a sweet, strong aroma and flavour.

47. Bean Blossoms

- **Common name :** Baybean
- **Scientific name :** *Canavalia Rosea*
- **Family :** Fabaceae
- **Native land :** Coastal areas of Australia, West Africa

It is a perennial herb with a trailing or climbing stem growing 2-10 metres long and becoming somewhat woody with age. Blooming takes place with the greatest intensity between May and September. The seeds are impermeable to water; thus they float considerable distances in the sea. The seeds serve as an important source of dietary protein in West Africa and Nigeria. The leaves, stems, and seeds have many nutritional and medicinal uses due to their high protein-content and active bactericidal ingredients. A paste of the leaves is used as a treatment for boils.

48. Beans–Lima

- **Common name :** Lima Bean, Butter Bean
- **Scientific name :** *Phaseolus lunatus*
- **Family :** Fabaceae
- **Native land :** Central and South America

Lima bean is a herbaceous perennial plant but is generally grown as an annual. The plant is bushy, which grows up to 3.25 feet. The white to yellow flowers, which occur in loose, open unbranched clusters develop into broad, flat pods up to 9 cm long. This species requires a long, warm growing season for bean development. This legume is valued for its edible seeds which are high in protein and have a good amount of some of vitamins and minerals as well. Lima beans have a number of medicinal uses, too.

49. Beans–Runner

- **Common name** : Runner Bean, Multiflora Bean
- **Scientific name** : *Phaseolus coccineus*
- **Family** : Fabaceae
- **Native land** : South America, Asia (Pakistan)

Runner beans are long, twining perennial vines that are usually grown as annuals for their showy flowers and their edible pods and seeds. The leaves are trifoliate and each leaflet is broad-oval. The flowers in most cultivars are bright scarlet red. Runner beans are more popular as food in Europe. The immature pods are used like green beans. The flowers are delicious as salads. The seeds in the shell stage are good to eat, but the mature beans are dry and mealy and are not generally consumed.

50. Beans–Snap

- **Common name** : Snap Bean, Green Bean, Kidney Bean
- **Scientific name** : *Phaseolus vulgaris*
- **Family** : Fabaceae
- **Native land** : Central and South America

It is a herbaceous annual plant, grown worldwide for its edible fruit, either the dry seed or the unripe fruit, both of which are referred to as beans. The plant has trifoliate compound leaves with oval to rhombic leaflets covered with downy hair. The flowers develop into linear round to slightly flattened pods. Green beans are high in vitamin C and dietary fibre. These are occasionally served fresh in salads but are more often prepared as a cooked vegetable. Green beans are often sold canned or frozen.

51. Beaucarnea

- **Common name** : Ponytail Palm, Elephant-foot Tree
- **Scientific name** : *Beaucarnea recurvata*
- **Family** : Asparagaceae
- **Native land** : Mexico and Central America.

Beaucarnea is an evergreen flowering perennial. The plant resembles a palm. It is a slow-growing plant with a green rosette of recurved, pendulous leaves rising from its swollen trunk. It has a greatly expanded base and a single trunk with a rosette of long, strap-like leaves. With age, the trunk eventually develops a few branches. It can grow up to 30 feet tall. It cannot resist cold temperatures, so in countries with strong winters it must be an indoor plant. The plant is also referred to as the elephant-foot tree because of the swollen shape of the base, coupled with the greyish-brown colour and the wrinkled texture of the bark. This species is often grown as a houseplant in temperate latitudes.

52. Beech

- **Common name :** Oriental Beech
- **Scientific name :** *Fagus orientalis*
- **Family :** Fagaceae
- **Native land :** Caucasus Mountains in Georgia, Azerbai-jan, and Armenia, Eastern Europe and Asia Minor

It is an evergreen annual deciduous broad-leaved tree. It can grow up to 100 feet tall. It has a smooth pale grey bark and obovate leaves. The leaves are alternate, simple and whole. Fruit maturation occurs in October, 5-6 months after pollination. The oriental beech is a fine shade tree for parks, estates and large lawns. The wood from the beech trees is close-grained and hard, and valued for flooring, furniture and construction. Beech nuts are a major source of food for wildlife.

53. Beets

- **Common name :** Beetroot
- **Scientific name :** *Beeta vulgaris*
- **Family :** Amaranthaceae
- **Native land :** Southern Europe

Beets are herbaceous biennial or, rarely, perennial plants. The leaves are simple and the petals or the sepals are fused into a cup or tube. The roots are most commonly deep red-purple in colour. Beets may be cooked for use as vegetables, pickled, added to salads, or made into the classic soup known as borscht. In Turkey, it is used as a medicinal herb by diabetic patients. The leaves are high in vitamin A and minerals including calcium, iron, potassium, and magnesium. Beetroots are high in magnesium and manganese, with some vitamin C.

54. Begonia

- **Common name :** Wax Begonia
- **Scientific name :** *Begonia obliqua*
- **Family :** Begoniaceae
- **Native land :** Mexico, Central and South America, Asia and South Africa

It grows in moist sub-tropical and tropical climates. It is an annual terrestrial herb or under shrub plant. This plant grows mostly in shaded spots in equatorial countries. Begonia is a frost-tender plant. The height of a plant ranges from 6-12 inches. The plant produces single or double one-inch flowers in red, white or pink. Wax begonias are good for mass planting, as hedging plants. The plants tolerate hot humid conditions well. Their bloom time is late spring to autumn.

55. Begonia Tubers

- **Common name** : Tuberous Begonia
- **Scientific name** : *Begonia tuberhybrida*
- **Family** : Begoniaceae
- **Native land** : Tropical South America and Southern Africa

Tuberous begonia is a flowering perennial plant. The plants generally grow 12-18 inches tall. Tuberous begonias grow best in a location that has partial to full shade, but bright light. Most tuberous begonias are bushy in stature, but some are trailing. These are grown mainly for their flowers. They contain brightly coloured waxy-petaled flowers. Tuberous begonias come in shades of white, pink, red, yellow, orange, and salmon, as well as bi-colours. Tuber hybrida begonias are used as bedding and border plants.

56. Beloperone Guttata

- **Common name** : Shrimp Plant
- **Scientific name** : *Justicia brandegeeana*
- **Family** : Acanthaceae
- **Native land** : Mexico, peninsular Florida

It is an evergreen perennial shrub. It is often grown in tropical and sub-tropical gardens. It grows only 2 to 3 feet tall but spreads up to 6 feet wide. Flower blooms almost throughout the year. The leaves are oval, light green and 5-8 cm long. The young stems and the undersides of the leaves are soft and downy. There are cultivars with yellow bracts, bright red bracts, and others with lime green bracts. The plant is used in mixed perennial beds and borders.

57. Berries

- **Common name** : Berries/Raspberries
- **Scientific name** : *Rubus occidentalis*
- **Family** : Rosaceae
- **Native land** : Eastern North America

Berries are found on low bushes and ground creepers. They are perennial with woody stems. There are about 450-500 species of berries. Habitats include openings in deciduous woodlands, woodland borders, savannas, thickets, fencerows, etc. They thrive mostly under partial sun. A few varieties of wild berries need cooking, but the most common and plentiful can be eaten fresh. Nutritionally, berries are a good source of vitamin C. The fruits are used in jams, preserves and various food products.

58. Billbergia

- **Common name** : Queen's Tears
- **Scientific name** : *Billbergia nutans*
- **Family** : Bromeliaceae
- **Native land** : Brazil, Venezuela, French Guiana, Lesser Antilles and Cuba

Billbergia is a perennial flowering ornamental houseplant. It grows on trees and on rocks or the ground in subtropical forests. It readily forms clumps of bronze-green leaf rosettes. The spikes of blue-green flowers are held on pink stems, providing dramatic colour contrasts. The leaf margins are usually finely toothed and the tip is pointed. They have small roots, mainly used for anchoring themselves on trees, so these tree-dwelling plants gather moisture and nutrients through their leaves.

59. Biophytum

- **Common name** : Little Tree Plant
- **Scientific name** : *Biophytum sensitivum*
- **Family** : Oxalidaceae
- **Native land** : Nepal, India and in other South-East Asian countries

It is a small, sensitive flowering annual herb which looks like a miniature palm. Its leaves are sensitive. It has unbranched stems up to 30 cm in height but usually shorter. The leaves are pinnately compounded, numerous, crowded at the apex of the stem, and 5-12 cm long, with 8-14 pairs of leaflets. It has several medicinal properties such as antioxidant activity, anti-inflammatory activity, wound healing, etc. During the national festival of Onam in Kerala, intricate and colourful arrangements of its flowers laid on the floor, called Pookalam, are made.

60. Birch

- **Common name** : Paper Birch
- **Scientific name** : *Betula papyrifera*
- **Family** : Betulaceae
- **Native land** : Cold climates of Canada and Alaska, and some parts of the Northern US states

Paper birch is a slender and graceful deciduous annual tree with white bark. The bark has a chalky covering that rubs off easily, and this is one way to distinguish this tree from other birches with white bark. It grows up to 70 feet tall. The leaves are alternate, ovate in shape. They are green-coloured with brown edges. The flowers are wind-pollinated catkins. It is usually cultivated for its highly ornamental bark which is especially attractive in winter, framed by its delicate lacy twigs.

221 Plants Enc

61. Black Locust

- **Common name :** Black Locust
- **Scientific name :** *Robinia pseudoacacia*
- **Family :** Fabaceae
- **Native land :** South-Eastern United States

Black locust is a medium-sized tree, growing up to 50 feet in height. The leaves are pinnately compound, and the oval-shaped leaflets are always paired. It has white blooms for only 10 days during spring, and black seedpods that are present on the tree throughout winter. The bark, seeds, and leaves of the black locust are all poisonous because it produces robin, an extremely potent phytotoxin. It is poisonous in both fresh and dried form, so people avoid tying horses to these trees or hitching posts made from its wood.

62. Black Currant

- **Common name :** Black Currant
- **Scientific name :** *Ribes nigrum*
- **Family :** Grossulariaceae
- **Native land :** Temperate parts of Central and Northern Europe and Northern Asia

It is a compact, mounding, deciduous shrub which grows up to 4 feet tall. The plant produces multi-seeded black berries up to 1 cm in size, which ripen in July and August. Clusters of greenish-yellow flowers bloom in spring, and are noticeable but not particularly ornamental. It is primarily for fruit production. Currants may be eaten fresh or used to make jams, jellies and pies. The leaves yield a yellow natural dye and the fruit yields a blue or violet natural dye.

63. Black-eyed Susan

- **Common name :** Black-eyed Susan
- **Scientific name :** *Rudbeckia hirta*
- **Family :** Asteraceae
Native land : The Eastern and Central United States

Black-eyed Susan, a wildflower, is categorised as an annual to a short-lived perennial across its range a flowering plant. It blooms in the first year from the seed planted in early spring, and is accordingly often grown as an annual. It typically occurs in open woods, prairies, fields, roadsides and waste areas. It is famous for its bright-yellow, daisy-like flowers with dark centres. The stems and scattered, oval leaves are covered with bristly hairs. Black-eyed Susan has been found to have immuno-stimulant activity. The juice squeezed from the roots is used for ear-aches.

33

64. Blechnum

- **Common name :** Deer Fern, Hard Fern
- **Scientific name :** *Blechnum spicant*
- **Family :** Blechnaceae
- **Native land :** Europe and Western North America

Blechnum is an evergreen fern. It can grow up to 1 feet tall. It is one of the plants grown in the woodland garden. It is an adaptable fern growing well in light to deep shade. This fern is particularly distinctive because of its two different types of fronds (a large leaf of a fern). They are fertile and sterile fronds (those that produce spores and those that do not, respectively). Fertile fronds turn brown and wither by the end of summer, leaving the evergreen sterile rosette.

65. Bletilla

- **Common name :** Chinese Ground Orchid
- **Scientific name :** *Bletilla striata*
- **Family :** Orchidaceae
- **Native land :** Japan, Korea, Nansei-shoto, Myanmar and China

Chinese ground orchid is a terrestrial orchid. It has thin, pleated leaves that resemble a small palm tree, and it produces about five flowers per stem. It produces small, pinkish-purple flowers. The flowers bloom mid-to-late spring. Bletilla species are generally hardy, though some need protection from severely cold frost. It is also used in herbal medicine. The rhizome (root) of this plant is known for its astringent, expectorant and emollient (due to the high mucus-content of the plant) properties and it has been used to treat indigestion, dysentery and fever.

66. Blue Fescue

- **Common name :** Blue Fescue
- **Scientific name :** *Festuca glauca 'Elijah Blue'*
- **Family :** Poaceae
- **Native land :** Europe

It is an evergreen or semi-evergreen herbaceous perennial grass. It is deep sea blue in colour. Blue fescue is a low-growing, semi-evergreen ornamental grass noted for its finely-textured, silver-blue foliage. Foliage forms a dome-shaped, porcupine-like tuft of erect needle-like blade radiating upward and outward. Light green flowers with a purple tinge appear above the foliage in late spring to early summer, but are not very showy. Blue fescue is very heat-tolerant. It is an excellent grass as ground cover, border front or rock garden accent, edging plant or container.

67. Blue Flag

- **Common name** : Blue Flag, German Iris
- **Scientific name** : *Iris germanica*
- **Family** : Iridaceae
- **Native land** : Southern Europe and the Mediterranean area

Blue flag is a perennial herbaceous flowering plant that is found in shallow water along shorelines and in wet areas. The plants grow up to 3 feet tall, with sword-shaped linear leaves and usually large fragrant blooms on stalks that branch below their midpoints. This plant possesses the unique ability to adapt to extreme environmental conditions, surviving in both desert and wetland areas. The extract from the roof of the iris helps the skin look and feel healthy, soft and supple.

68. Borage

- **Common name** : Starflower/Bee Plant/Bee Bread
- **Scientific name** : *Borago officinalis*
- **Family** : Boraginaceae
- **Native land** : Mediterranean region

Starflower is a flowering annual herb. Borage has blue purplish star-shaped flowers that attract bees all summer long. It grows up to 3.3 feet tall. The stem and the leaves have hairy texture. The flowers are most often blue in colour. The leaves are edible. The plant is also commercially cultivated for the seed oil extracted from its seeds. It is cultivated and used widely throughout Europe for its healing properties and for a nice addition to salads. Its anti-inflammatory properties help soothe the irritated skin while helping it retain moisture and elasticity.

69. Bougainvillea

- **Common name** : Great Bougainvillea
- **Scientific name** : *Bougainvillea spectabilis*
- **Family** : Nyctaginaceae
- **Native land** : South America from Brazil west to Peru and south to southern Argentina, South-East Asia

Bougainvillea is evergreen in regions experiencing rainfall throughout the year, and deciduous where a dry season occurs. It is a thorny perennial vine, with stout spines. The leaves are alternate, simple, ovate to somewhat elliptic. The flowers arise in leaf axils, in clusters of threes (purple, red, pink, or orange). This species is used as an ornamental plant. It is adapted to climates with a distinct dry season and does not flower well in perpetually humid conditions.

70. Bouvardia

- **Common name :** Firecracker Bush/Trumpetellia/Hummingbird Flower
- **Scientific name :** *Bouvardia ternifolia*
- **Family :** Rubiaceae
- **Native land :** Mexico and Central America

Bouvardia is an evergreen flowering shrubby perennial. Bouvardia typically blooms between May and October, and can live up to 10 years. The plant grows up to 1.5 metres tall. The leaves are bright green and pointed. Bouvardia comes in the shades of white, pink, salmon, and red. Several species of bouvardia are grown as ornamental plants, both in the tropics and indoors as houseplants in temperate regions. It is used as remedy to treat patients who have been stung by scorpions.

71. Brassica Flowers

- **Common name :** Brassica Flowers, Ornamental Cabbage, Kale
- **Scientific name :** *Brassica oleracea*
- **Family :** Brassicaceae
- **Native land :** Coastal Southern and Western Europe

Brassica is a herbaceous annual, biennial, or occasionally perennial with smooth, glaucous (waxy), rounded lower leaves. This genus includes the cabbages and the mustards. It is a cool weather vegetable that is grown for the harvest of its edible leaves. Cabbage forms heads and kale forms upright leaves. The leaf colours are usually quite showy, including white/cream, pink, rose, red and purple. Cabbage and kale are in the same species as a number of other cool season vegetables, including Brussels sprouts, broccoli, cauliflower and kohlrabi.

72. Browallia

- **Common name :** Bush Violet, Jamaican Forget-me-not
- **Scientific name :** *Browallia americana*
- **Family :** Solanaceae
- **Native land :** Tropical Latin America, from Mexico and the Caribbean, south to Peru and Brazil

Browallia is a true annual flowering plant. Browallia is a bushy plant that fills the gaps in the garden with bright, sky-blue flowers. The plants grow up to 2 feet tall. This plant produces distinct, 2-inch blossoms primarily in rich blue with dark eyes smudged white. It requires the sun and partial shade for proper growth. Its flowers are a deep lilac-blue upon opening, but they fade to mauve. Browallia seeds make a great addition to the summer flowerbed in the garden.

73. Brunfelsia

- **Common name :** Brazil Raintree, Morning-noon-and-night, Yesterday-today-and-tomorrow
- **Scientific name :** *Brunfelsia pauciflora*
- **Family :** Solanaceae
- **Native land :** Woodland areas of Brazil

Brunfelsia is a deciduous or evergreen woody perennial. It grows up to 8 feet tall with several stems. The leaves are leathery and semi-evergreen, dark green above and pale beneath. The fragrant, pansy-like flowers with white throats last for three days and change colour with each day. The flowers start out purple, gradually fade to lavender and then white. The flowers of all three colours are present throughout the blooming season. The fruit of the plant is toxic. Titrated doses of root are highly recommended in the treatment of chronic rheumatism of an arthritic nature. The plant is used mainly for ornamental use.

74. Brussels Sprout

- **Common name :** Brussels sprout
- **Scientific name :** *Brassica oleracea* (Gemmifera Group)
- **Family :** Brassicaceae
- **Native land :** Belgium

Brassica oleracea is a herbaceous annual plant. Brussels sprout is a slow-growing, long-season vegetable crop. It reportedly won its name after becoming popular in Brussels, Belgium, in the 1200s. It is a cool weather vegetable that is grown for the harvest of miniature cabbage-like buds. The sprout is produced in the leaf axils, starting at the base of the stem and working upward. Its colour ranges from light green to red or purple. Brussels sprout is an excellent source of vitamins A, C, K, folic acid, minerals and fibre. It is proven that Brussels sprout can prevent various cancerous tumours.

75. Buckwheat

- **Common name :** Buckwheat
- **Scientific name :** *Fagopyrum esculentum*
- **Family :** Polygonaceae
- **Native land :** China

Buckwheat is a herbaceous annual plant. Buckwheat is not a cereal grain, but is actually a fruit seed. It is native to China, but now commonly cultivated in Bhutan, Korea, Mongolia, Myanmar, Nepal, Russia and Sikkim; also Australia, Europe and North America. Buckwheat is a short season crop. It begins to flower in four weeks and produces grains in 8 to 12 weeks. The plant can grow up to 10 feet tall. The stems of the plant are bare and branching; the leaves are alternate and sagittate-triangular. The flowers range from white to red in colour and have a pungent odour. Buckwheat is sometimes used as a green manure, as erosion control, or as wildlife cover and feed.

76. Burdock

- **Common name** : Burdock, Common Weed
- **Scientific name** : *Burdock arctium*
- **Family** : Asteraceae
- **Native land** : Europe and Northern Asia

Burdock is a biennial herbaceous plant. This plant grows relatively tall; therefore, it has deep roots which are brownish green, or nearly black on the outside. Its leaves are large, wavy, heart-shaped and green in colour. The leafstalks are generally hollow. Arctium species generally flower from July through to October. The taproot of young burdock plants can be harvested and eaten as a root vegetable. In Europe, burdock root was used as a bittering agent in beer before the widespread adoption of hops for this purpose.

77. Buttercup

- **Common name** : California Buttercup
- **Scientific name** : *Ranunculus californicus*
- **Family** : Ranunculaceae
- **Native land** : California

California buttercup is a flowering perennial. It grows up to 3 feet tall. The numerous stems sprawl to erect 15 to 50 cm long. The stems generally have several shiny, lemon-yellow flowers in an open inflorescence. The flowers have up to 16 petals. The seeds of California buttercup are usually ground into a powder and used to flavour soups, or mixed with cereals while making bread etc. However, livestock grazing on this plant suffer from paralysis.

78. Buxus

- **Common name** : Winter Gem Boxwood, Korean Boxwood
- **Scientific name** : *Buxus sinica var. insularis*
- **Family** : Buxaceae
- **Native land** : Southern and Eastern Asia, British Isles

Buxus is an evergreen broadleaf shrub. It is very compact, grows wider than tall, and the annual growth rate is about 25 mm. This plant is extremely hardy and is a good choice for northern climates. The greenish yellow flowers appear in early spring. The fruit is inconspicuous. The flowers are insignificant but quite fragrant. The leaves are small, obovate, medium and green in colour. Boxwoods have lots of utility in the garden. They are ideal for formal hedges and foundation plantings. They are also excellent plants for bonsai and topiary.

79. Calendula

- **Common name** : Calendula, Pot Marigold, Field Marigold
- **Scientific name** : *Calendula arvensis*
- **Family** : Asteraceae
- **Native land** : Central and Southern Europe

Calendula is an annual and perennial herbaceous plant. It grows among the long grass of fields and displays its golden flowers from spring to autumn and again in winter if the weather is mild. The name calendula refers to the almost all-year blooming. The leaves are lance-shaped and borne on petioles from the slender, hairy stem. The oil made with the flower heads of Calendula arvensis have been used to treat wounds and skin irritations in the Mediterranean region since ancient Greeks. It has been used medicinally worldwide.

80. Calla Lily

- **Common name** : White Calla Lily, Arum Lily
- **Scientific name** : *Zantedeschia aethiopica*
- **Family** : Araceae
- **Native land** : Southern Africa in Lesotho, South Africa, and Swaziland

It is a rhizomatous herbaceous perennial plant, evergreen in wet and warm regions and deciduous where there is a dry season. Calla lilies are not true lilies; its brilliant white floral bract surround the central pale yellow floral spike bearing tiny flowers. They are stemless plants whose flowers and leaves rise directly from the rhizomes. The arrow-shaped leaves are bright green. The plant grows up to 3 feet tall. All parts of the plant are poisonous, causing irritation and swelling of the mouth and acute gastric diarrhoea.

81. Campanula

- **Common name** : Serbian Bellflower
- **Scientific name** : *Campanula poscharskyana*
- **Family** : Campanulaceae
- **Native land** : Mountains of Bosnia, Croatia

It is a semi evergreen, trailing perennial flower. The name campanula refers to the shape of the flowers. Campanula blooms at a height of 0.25 to 0.75 feet with blue, indigo and violet flowers. It spreads quickly to form dense blankets of dainty, star-shaped lilac-blue blooms with white centres. It is a creeping perennial, perfect for rock gardens or sunny rock walls. It prefers moist, well-drained soil, but can tolerate drier conditions as well. The bloom time is May to June.

82. Caragana

- **Common name** : Siberian Pea Tree
- **Scientific name** : *Caragana arborescens*
- **Family** : Fabaceae
- **Native land** : Eastern Russia, Northern China

It is a perennial shrub. Siberian pea tree is a large, rounded, multi-stemmed, deciduous shrub with upright branching that grows up to 15-20 feet tall and to 12-15 feet wide. The leaves are bright green, each with 4 to 6 pairs of leaflets. The stipules are usually spiny. The pea-like yellow flowers bloom singly or in clusters in May. The flowers give way to yellowish-green pods that mature to brown in summer. The caragana has a fragrant flower that will naturally attract bees. The honey created has a pleasant taste, slightly 'fruity'.

83. Cardamom

- **Common name** : Cardamom/Choti Elaichi
- **Scientific name** : *Elettaria cardamomum*
- **Family** : Zingiberaceae
- **Native land** : India

Cardamom is a herbaceous perennial plant. It is a bushy herb that grows to a height of 6 to10 feet with erect shoots. It has a large, fleshy rhizome. The leaves are long, alternate and lance-shaped. The flowers are small and usually yellowish in colour with a violet lip. The fruits are thin-walled, smooth-skinned, oblong capsules. Each fruit contains aromatic reddish brown seeds. Its warming property relieves cough and headache resulting from cold weather. Cardamom is a principal ingredient in curry powders, and is used to flavour confectioneries, liqueurs and chewing gums. It is the world's third-most expensive spice.

84. Cardoon

- **Common name** : Cardoon
- **Scientific name** : *Cynara cardunculus*
- **Family** : Asteraceae
- **Native land** : Western and Central Mediterranean region

It is a perennial plant. It can reach up to 5 feet tall and spread up to 4 feet wide. Cardoon requires a long, cool growing season, but is a frost-sensitive plant. It typically requires substantial growing space per plant, so is not much grown except where it is regionally popular. The plant is also grown as an ornamental plant for its imposing architectural appearance, with very bright silvery-grey foliage and large flowers in selected cultivars. Edible leafstalks and midribs are tasty when blanched. Unopened flowerheads can be eaten like artichokes.

85. Carrot

- **Common name :** Carrot
- **Scientific name :** *Daucus carota*
- **Family :** Apiaceae
- **Native land :** Europe and South-Western Asia

The carrot is a herbaceous variable biennial plant. It grows up to 2 feet tall. It has delicate white flower heads. It has a thin, wiry taproot that is fleshy, bright orange root vegetable. The orange colour of a cultivated carrot is due to a high concentration of beta-carotene. This is a precursor of vitamin A, which is important for growth, development and good vision. Carrots are eaten raw or briefly cooked. The spiny fruits have been considered to have diuretic properties, and have been used in the treatment of kidney complaints and dropsy.

86. Castor Bean

- **Common name :** Castor Oil Plant
- **Scientific name :** *Ricinus communis*
- **Family :** Euphorbiaceae
- **Native land :** Tropics (Africa)

Castor bean is a herbaceous annual which can grow up to nearly 15 feet tall when grown in open spaces and warm climates. The leaves are glossy and often red or bronze tinted when young. The flowers appear in clusters at the end of the main stem in late summer. The fruit consists of an oblong spiny pod which contains three seeds on average. The plant itself is fast growing, but the seeds require a long frost-free season in order to mature. All parts are highly toxic if ingested.

87. Catananche

- **Common name :** Cupid's Dart
- **Scientific name :** *Catananche caerulea*
- **Family :** Asteraceae
- **Native land :** Mediterranean region

It is a short-lived perennial. The bright blue, cornflower-like blooms of catananche appear continuously from early to late summer and are at their peak in midsummer. They grow in full sun. The plant is rather narrow and upright with little foliage. Its papery petals have a fine silvery stripe through the centre. The flower is also used in dry flower arrangements. The plant provides plenty of bloom from the first year of planting.

88. Cauliflower

- **Common name** : Romanesco Broccoli, Cauliflower
- **Scientific name** : *Brassica oleracea* (Botrytis Group)
- **Family** : Brassicaceae
- **Native land** : Western Europe

A cauliflower is an annual vegetable that is reproduced by seeds. It is a cool weather vegetable. The edible portion of a cauliflower is a curd-like mass composed of a close aggregation of abortive flowers developed on the thick bunches of the inflorescence. The colour of the leaf is often lighter green. Winter or late-season types have curds that consist of functional flower buds, similar to broccoli. Purple cauliflower is a winter variety of broccoli. If harvested before frost, the heads taste like broccoli; after frost, the heads taste like cauliflower. Purple cauliflower turns green when cooked.

89. Centranthus

- **Common name** : Red Valerian, Jupiter's Beard, Keys of Heaven, Fox's Bush
- **Scientific name** : *Centranthus ruber*
- **Family** : Valerianaceae
- **Native land** : South of England

The rootstock is perennial and very freely branching, enabling it to take a firm hold in the crevices in which it has once gained possession. The stems are stout, somewhat shrubby at the base, between 1 and 2 feet long, hollow and very smooth in texture. Both leaves and roots can be eaten, the leaves either fresh in salads or lightly boiled, the roots boiled in soups. It flowers the first year when grown from seed, and makes a great cut flower.

90. Chamomile

- **Common name** : Chamomile
- **Scientific name** : *Matricaria chamomilla*
- **Family** : Asteraceae
- **Native land** : Europe, including Britain, East to west and Asia and the Himalayas

The root is perennial, jointed and fibrous. The stems, hairy and freely branching, are covered with leaves that are divided into thread-like segments. It blooms from June to July, and the seeds ripen from July to August. The plant can grow up to 2 feet in height. The young springs are used as a seasoning. The dried flowers are used to make herbal teas. It is aromatic but with a very bitter flavour. Historically, it has been used to treat many conditions, including digestive problems, chest colds, sore throats, abscesses, gum inflammation, anxiety, etc.

91. Chard

- **Common name :** Swiss Chard
- **Scientific name :** *Beta vulgaris* (Cicla Group)
- **Family :** Amaranthaceae
- **Native land :** Europe, North Africa and Western Asia

Swiss chard is an annual leafy garden vegetable that is closely related to beets. It is largely distinguished from the beets by its lack of enlarged fleshy underground roots. Swiss chard typically forms a dense rosette of upright-arching, crumpled, glossy, medium green leaves, each having distinctive midribs and long, broad, colourful crisp leafstalks. Both the leafstalks (petioles) and the leaves are edible. It is a good substitute for spinach.

92. Chervil

- **Common name :** Chervil
- **Scientific name :** *Anthriscus cerefolium*
- **Family :** Apiaceae or Umbelliferae
- **Native land :** South-Eastern Europe, Britain

It is an upright annual with aniseed-flavoured, 2- to 3-pinnate leaves with ovate leaflets, and umbels of small white flowers in summer. They grow up to 0.1-0.5 metre. The finely-cut, bright green leaves can be used as a fresh and spicy alternative to parsley for everyday dishes such as mashed potatoes and scrambled eggs. The leaves should always be used fresh because the delicate flavour does not withstand drying or prolonged cooking. The flowers and the roots of the plant are also edible.

93. Chinese Hibiscus

- **Common name :** Hawaiian hibiscus or rose of China
- **Scientific name :** *Hibiscus rosa-sinensis*
- **Family :** Malvaceae
- **Native land :** Asia and tropical Africa

It is an annual herbaceous shrub. The plant is about 3.5 metres tall and has a deep penetrating tap root. The dark green, toothed leaves are arranged alternately on the branches. Flowers are borne singly in the leaf axils. The flowers are red to dark red. The bloom time is in summer and autumn. This plant attracts hummingbirds and butterflies. The flower extract has been traditionally used for liver disorders and high blood pressure. Hibiscus tea is rich in Vitamin C. The fruit is used externally in cases of sprains, wounds and ulcers.

94. Chives

- **Common name :** Chives
- **Scientific name :** *Allium schoenoprasum*
- **Family :** Amaryllidaceae (onion)
- **Native land :** Europe, Asia and North America

Allium schoenoprasum is a bulbous perennial, forming a clump of erect, narrowly cylindrical, onion-scented leaves, with rounded umbels of light purple bell-shaped flowers. They grow from 6 to 10 inches high. The flowers bloom in June and July. The Asian variety of chive is called Chinese chives, garlic chives or kuchai. Nutritionally, it is rich in vitamin C, potassium and folic acid. It is known to promote good digestion, ease stomach upset and prevent bad breath. It has a diuretic effect that will lower high blood pressure.

95. Cilantro/Coriander

- **Common name :** Cilantro
- **Scientific name :** *Coriandrum Sativum*
- **Family :** Apiaceae
- **Native land :** Southern Europe and the Western Mediterranean

It is a warm weather annual herb. It is commonly grown in herb gardens for its lacy, strong-scented foliage (cilantro) and its aromatic seeds (coriander). It has slender stems with leaves on it. The leaves are larger at the base and at the top tips of the branches they are a bit feathery in shape. Coriander is considered an aid to the digestive system. It is an appetite stimulant, and aids in the secretion of gastric juices. In India, it is used as one of the basic spices in food preparation.

96. Cleavers

- **Common name :** Cleavers
- **Scientific name :** *Galium aparine*
- **Family :** Rubiaceae
- **Native land :** Europe and Western Asia (i.e. Eurasia), Australia

Cleavers is an annual, sprawling herb. It has small hooks along the stems, at the tip and along the edges of the leaves and on the fruit. These hooks will catch (cleave) onto clothes, fur and feathers, helping this plant to spread to new locations. The leaves are lance-shaped, with the apex or tip broadly rounded. The flowers are small and appear on a short straight stem. The fruit is kidney-shaped, densely covered with hooked hair on a straight pedicel (flower stalk). The leaves and the stems of the plant can be cooked as a leaf vegetable if gathered before the fruits appear.

97. Clematis

- **Common name** : Clematis
- **Scientific name** : *Clematis triternata rubromarginata*
- **Family** : Ranunculaceae
- **Native land** : Eastern North America, including Missouri

Clematis is an evergreen herbaceous perennial vine. The almond-scented, star-shaped flowers are violet-pink or wine-coloured on the tips, fading to white at the base. A tuft of creamy yellow anthers with greenish connectives can been seen at the centre of the flowers. It is great for filling up a bare fence. Clematis blooms abundant flowers in the late spring followed by silvery grey seed heads. This vigorous climber is ideal for walls and fences, cottage gardens, scented gardens.

98. Clove Currant

- **Common name** : Clove Currant
- **Scientific name** : *Ribes odoratum*
- **Family** : Grossulariaceae
- **Native land** : Central United States

The clove currant is a loosely-branched, irregularly-shaped, perennial deciduous shrub. This plant grows upto 6-8 feet tall. This plant grows in many types of habitats, including rocky bluffs and slopes, and also along the sides of streams. It prefers rich, fertile, medium moisture, well-drained soil. The raw fruit is eaten by Native Americans and used in making pemmican. The fresh fruits are used for preparing jelly and jam. The leaves can be used to make tea or to flavour foods. The extracts of some Ribes species are toxic to various insects and pests.

99. Clover

- **Common name** : White Clover
- **Scientific name** : *Trifolium repens*
- **Family** : Fabaceae
- **Native land** : Temperate and sub-tropical regions (except South-East Asia and Australia)

White clover is an evergreen perennial plant. It grows up to 6 feet tall. White clover grows among turf grass, crops, and in a large number of other landscapes. It produces several compound leaves from a short stem initially, that grows only a little after which this stem rapidly elongates and becomes up to 1 feet long. These elongated stems sprawl along the ground and have the capacity to root at the nodes. They are hairless and light green. The alternate compound leaves are trifoliate and hairless. This is the familiar clover in lawns with white flowerheads.

100. Collard Greens

- **Common name :** Collards
- **Scientific name :** *Brassica oleracea var. acephala*
- **Family :** Brassicaceae
- **Native land :** Coastal Southern and Western Europe

Collards is a biennial where winter frost occurs, and perennial in even colder regions. The plant (also known as tree-cabbage or non-heading cabbage) is a cool-season vegetable green that is rich in vitamins and minerals. It grows better in warm weather and can tolerate more cold weather in late autumn than any other member of the cabbage family. Although collards is a popular substitute for cabbage in Southern Europe yet it can also be grown in northern areas because it is frost-tolerant.

101. Comfrey

- **Common name :** Russian Comfrey
- **Scientific name :** *Symphytum uplandicum*
- **Family :** Boraginaceae
- **Native land :** Europe

Comfrey is a cultivated perennial herb. The plant grows up to 1 metre tall. Its leaves add relatively high amounts of nitrogen, potassium and phosphorus to the compost pile. It has lance-shaped, hairy leaves, hairy stems and magenta-pink flowers. The tubular pink flowers are in bud, turning mauve or blue and blooms from May to August. The plant can be harvested for both leaves and tubers. Comfrey has been used for thousands of years as a medicinal herb. The plant is now often grown specifically for its great usefulness as a fertiliser.

102. Coreopsis

- **Common name :** Tickseed, Thread Leaf Coreopsis
- **Scientific name :** *Coreopsis verticillata*
- **Family :** Asteraceae
- **Native land :** Eastern United States

Coreopsis is a herbaceous perennial wildflower that typically grows in dense, bushy clumps. It grows up to 3 feet tall. The flowers appear singly in loose clusters in a profuse and lengthy late spring to late summer bloom. Shearing plants in mid-summer will promote an autumn rebloom. The leaves of thread leaf coreopsis are very fine and divided into thread-like segments. The plant is beautiful with its fine foliage even if it never flowered. The flowers are abundant and bloom continuously throughout the entire summer.

103. Cucumber (Lemon Cucumber)

- **Common name :** Lemon Cucumber
- **Scientific name :** *Cucumis sativus*
- **Family :** Cucurbitaceae
- **Native land :** East Indies

Lemon cucumber is an annual vining cucumber plant. The plant can grow up to 0.75 to 1.50 feet tall. It performs best in full sun. The fruit is apple-shaped with lemon-yellow skin, and is extremely sweet. Resembling a lemon in colour, size and shape, the white flesh of lemon cucumber is sweet with a superb crunch. The lemon cucumber produces its first ripe fruits within 55 to 65 days of planting when given proper care and growing conditions. Just like a kiwi, the skin of lemon cucumber has tiny bristles that are edible. It is commonly used in a variety of ways, including raw in salads, pickled, sliced, stir fried and in soups.

104. Culinary Sage

- **Common name :** Common Sage
- **Scientific name :** *Salvia officinalis*
- **Family :** Lamiaceae
- **Native land :** Mediterranean (Iberia and Balkans) and Northern Africa

Common Sage is a shrubby, perennial plant that grows to about 2-3 feet tall. Its foliage is grey-green with a pebbly texture. As it ages, it has a tendency to sprawl. The spikes of purple flowers appear in mid-summer. It also has excellent ornamental qualities. The plant has whorls of two-lipped, lavender-blue flowers in short, upright spikes in late spring. Wrinkled, grey-green leaves are strongly aromatic and are frequently used fresh or dried in cooking as a seasoning. It is attractive to bees and butterflies. It is a standard herb garden plant.

105. Cumin

- **Common name :** Cumin
- **Scientific name :** *Cuminum cyminum*
- **Family :** Apiaceae
- **Native land :** East Mediterranean to India

Cumin is warm season, annual herbaceous plant. It grows up to 30-50 cm. It has a slender, glabrous, branched stem which is 20-30 cm tall. The stem is grey or dark green coloured. The leaves are 5-10 cm long with thread-like leaflets. The flowers are small, white or pink, and borne in umbels. Cumin seeds resemble caraway seeds, being oblong in shape, longitudinally ridged, and yellow-brown in colour. They are an excellent source of iron, manganese, calcium, magnesium, phosphorus and vitamin B1. Cumin is used to treat stomach upset and flatulence.

106. Daffodil

- **Common name** : Trumpet-Flowered Narcissus
- **Scientific name** : *Narcissus sp. Jonquilla*
- **Family** : Amaryllidaceae
- **Native land** : Mediterranean region, Northern Africa and Middle East

Daffodils are perennials. They bloom from March to May. These daffodils have blooms with flattened outer petals and trumpet-shaped cups that flare from their base to a wide, open rim. The flowers come in a wide variety of shades of red, orange, yellow, green, white, and pink. The bulbs of the daffodil as well as every other part of the plant are powerfully emetic, and the flowers are considered slightly poisonous, especially for children. In France, Narcissus flowers have been used as an anti-spasmodic.

107. Daisy

- **Common name** : Ox-eye Daisy
- **Scientific name** : *Chrysanthemum leucanthemum*
- **Family** : Compositae/Asteraceae
- **Native land** : Europe, Russia

Daisies are robust herbaceous perennials with narrowly oblong leaves and daisy-like flower-heads with white rays. The plant generally grows from 1 to 2 feet high. The stems are hard and wiry, furrowed and only very slightly branched. The leaves are small and coarsely toothed; those near the roots are somewhat rounder in form than those on the stem, and are on long stalks. Bloom period is from May to June. The taste of the dried herb is bitter and tingling. The young leaves are said to be eaten in salads in Italy.

108. Delosperma-ice

- **Common name** : Trailing Iceplant, Pink Carpet
- **Scientific name** : *Delosperma cooperi*
- **Family** : Aizoaceae
- **Native land** : Southern Africa

The iceplant is a herbaceous perennial plant. This species forms a low mat of succulent, shiny and cylindrical evergreen leaves, bearing loads of small, starry flowers in early summer, then on and off through the season. The daisy-like flowers are fluorescent purple in colour. Due to the low need for maintenance, it is suitable for urban environments and high temperature regions. The leaves take on a reddish colour in winter.
A single plant can spread up to 2 feet wide in one season. The plant grows up to 2 to 4 inches in height. Iceplant grows and spreads quickly, making it an ideal ground cover.

109. Delphinium

- **Common name** : Field Larkspur, Knight's Spur
- **Scientific name** : *Delphinium consolida*
- **Family** : Ranunculacae
- **Native land** : England, Europe

Delphinium is a long-stemmed perennial that typically grows to 4-6 feet tall. Some varieties are annuals, too. In late spring to early summer, the plant produces 3-inch double flowers densely packed into terminal spikes. The flowers are in short racemes, pink, purple or blue. The seeds are poisonous and have an acrid and bitter taste. They are dangerous, and cause vomiting and purging if eaten. Earlier, the juice of the flowers and an infusion of the whole plant were also prescribed against colic.

110. Dianthus

- **Common name** : Sweet William
- **Scientific name** : *Dianthus barbatus*
- **Family** : Caryophyllaceae
- **Native land** : Southern Europe from Pyrenees to Carpathians and Balkans

This is a short-lived perennial; it is also best grown as a biennial. The plant typically grows 1-2 feet tall and features small flowers held in dense, flat-topped terminal clusters. The plant prefers full sun, but may tolerate light shade. The flowers are held erect on long, upright stems over a compact mound of blue-green foliage. The plant attracts hummingbirds and butterflies. In ancient cultures, the petals of Sweet William were added to wine or vinegar to create a tonic that would sooth the nerves.

111. Dierama-wandflower

- **Common name** : Angel's Fishing Rods
- **Scientific name** : *Dierama dracomontanum*
- **Family** : Iridaceae
- **Native land** : South Africa

Wandflower is a cormous perennial that produces a clump of grass-like leaves and arching wiry flower stems topped by the spikes of pendulous bell-shaped flowers. The flowers range from shades of brick-pink to purple. The North American varieties are mostly purple to pink in colour. The bloom period is from June to August. The plant is evergreen, although it dies back in winter months and goes through a rest period. It attracts birds, butterflies and bees.

112. Dill

- **Common name :** Dill Seeds
- **Scientific name :** *Anethum graveolens*
- **Family :** Apiaceae
- **Native land :** South-Western Asia and India

Dill is a hardy annual herb. It is commonly grown for the culinary attributes of its leaves and seeds. The plant grows ordinarily from 2.0 to 2.5 feet high and is very much like fennel. It provides a valuable food source for a butterfly's larvae and attracts insects as well. The French use Dill seeds for flavouring cakes and pastry, as well as for flavouring sauces. Dill vinegar, however, forms a popular household condiment. It is made by soaking the seeds in vinegar for a few days before using.

113. Doll's Eyes

- **Common name :** Doll's Eyes/White Baneberry
- **Scientific name :** *Actaea pachypoda*
- **Family :** Ranunculacea
- **Native land :** Yorkshire and the Lake District

It is a herbaceous perennial plant. The name Doll's Eye originates from its white spherical berries with black dots on the tip. The flowers are in oblong clusters on thick, red stalks. The leaflets have sharp teeth. Its leaves are twice-divided. The fruits present from May through October. The entire plant is poisonous to mankind and has been ranked as one of the top ten most deadly plants in the US. Strangely, the berries are said to be harmless to birds.

114. Duck Potato

- **Common name :** Broadleaf Arrowhead
- **Scientific name :** *Sagittaria latifolia*
- **Family :** Alismataceae
- **Native land :** Europe and Northern Asia, as well as North America

It is a vigorous, deciduous, marginal aquatic perennial that typically grows up to 1 to 4 feet tall. The leaves are borne on triangular stalks that vary in length. The flower-stem rises directly from the root and bears several rings of buds and blossoms. The stem is swollen at the base and produces globose winter tubers (composed almost entirely of starch). The tubers are also an important food source for waterfowl, hence the name duck potato. The seeds are attractive to many water birds. Arrowhead is commonly used in pond restorations.

115. Dusty Miller

- **Common name :** Dusty Miller
- **Scientific name :** *Cineraria maritima*
- **Family :** Asteraceae (Compositae)
- **Native land :** Shores of the Mediterranean

It is an annual evergreen shrub. The unusual silvery grey/white foliage of this plant provides attractive contrast to bold-coloured garden flowers. It prefers summers that are warm and dry and winters that are cool (not cold) and wet. Its leaves can be entire, deeply lobed, or intricately lacy. The yellow flowers are attractive, but usually removed to prevent legginess and focus attention on foliage. The fresh juice is said to remove cataract though not recommended. This plant is excellent for edging borders and beds. The plant contains poisonous alkaloids and should not be eaten.

116. Elderberry

- **Common name :** Black Elder
- **Scientific name :** *Sambucus nigra*
- **Family :** Adoxaceae (Caprifoliaceae)
- **Native land :** Europe, North America

Elderberry is a deciduous multi-stemmed shrub with brittle branches that easily bent under the weight of its fruit clusters. It can reach up to 9 metres in height. It flowers in late June; the crop is seldom damaged by late spring frost. Elderberry fruit is harvested in late August through early September. Elderberries are popular for their unusual taste in pies, jellies and jams. They are occasionally used in winemaking. Elder leaves are used in the preparation of an ointment, which is a domestic remedy for bruises, sprains, chilblains and as an emollient.

117. Endive

- **Common name :** Endive (Salad Greens)/Escarole
- **Scientific name :** *Cichorium endivia*
- **Family :** Compositae/Asteraceae
- **Native land :** Egypt, Europe

It is an edible annual leafy plant. Endive grows as a loose head or rosette of leaves that are extremely curled and serrated. The plant requires rich light, well-drained, unshaded soil. When sown late in the season, it behaves as a biennial. In cultivation, the endive leaves are sometimes tied together in such a way that light cannot strike them. This causes the leaves to become blanched (turn white), removing the bitter taste of the green leaf. There are two main varieties: one with narrow, curled leaves; the other with broad, ragged leaves. The broad-leaved variety is also called escarole.

118. Erigeron

- **Common name :** Eastern Daisy
- **Scientific name :** *Erigeron annuus*
- **Family :** Asteraceae
- **Native land :** North America, Central Europe

It is an annual/perennial plant, growing at a medium rate. The plant grows up to 8-12 inches tall. Each plant has several composite flowers that look typically daisy-like, having a yellow central disk surrounded by white, petal-like rays. Composite flowers are positioned singularly atop the terminal shoot of downy stems. The leaves are also hairy, lanceolate, and coarsely toothed. Bloom time varies from summer to mid-autumn. The leaves when bruised have a somewhat soap-like smell. The sap that lies in the tissues is bitter, astringent and salty. Animals do not generally eat the plant.

119. Feijoa

- **Common name :** Feijoa Sellowiana, Pineapple Guava
- **Scientific name :** *Acca sellowiana*
- **Family :** Myrtaceae
- **Native land :** Highlands of Southern Brazil, Eastern Paraguay, Uruguay, Northern Argentina, and Colombia

Feijoa is a grey-green multi-stemmed evergreen shrub or small tree. It can grow up to 3-6 metres tall. The plants can be pruned to form a hedge or a small tree. The plant can withstand several degrees below freezing. The stiff shiny green leaves are lighter underneath and very showy flowers are produced from April to June. They have long, scarlet stamens topped with large grains of yellow pollen. The fresh fruit is widely consumed because of its characteristic flavour and aroma, which are similar to a pineapple.

120. Fennel

- **Common name :** Fennel
- **Scientific name :** *Foeniculum vulgare*
- **Family :** Apiaceae
- **Native land :** Southern Europe and the Mediterranean region

Fennel is a biennial, hardy, perennial–umbelliferous herb with yellow flowers and feathery leaves. It grows to a height of up to 2.5 metres with hollow stems. The leaves are finely dissected. The flowers are produced in terminal compound umbels. The fruit is a dry seed about 4-10 mm long. It is a highly aromatic and flavourful herb with culinary and medicinal uses. In aroma, fennel seeds are like anise and are used as flavouring in baked goods, meat and fish dishes, ice cream, alcoholic beverages and herb mixtures.

121. Fenugreek

- **Common name :** Fenugreek
- **Scientific name :** *Trigonella foenum-graecum*
- **Family :** Fabacecae
- **Native land :** Eastern Mediterranean

Fenugreek is an annual herb indigenous to the countries bordering on the eastern shores of the Mediterranean and largely cultivated in India, Egypt and Morocco. The plant grows up to 3 feet tall, and has three-part leaves. The long slender stems bear tripartite, toothed, grey-green obovate leaves, 20-25 mm long. The flowering season for fenugreek is generally midsummer. The fruit is a curved seed-pod, with ten to twenty flat and hard, yellowish-brown seeds. Dried or fresh leaves of fenugreek are used as herb, seeds as spice, and fresh leaves as vegetable. Sotolon is the chemical responsible for the distinctive sweet smell of this herb.

122. Four o'clock

- **Common name :** Four o'clock, Marvel-of-Peru, Beauty-of-the-night
- **Scientific name :** *Mirabilis jalapa*
- **Family :** Nyctaginaceae
- **Native land :** Tropical America

Four o'clock is an ornamental perennial plant. The plant is called four o'clock because its flowers, from white and yellow to shades of pink and red, sometimes streaked and mottled, open in late afternoon (and close by morning). The leaves are oval. The stems are swollen at the joints. The plants continue to produce new flowers from late spring until autumn. It has large, black carrot-shaped tubers that can be a foot or more long. A very important and curious aspect of this plant is that the flowers with different colours can be found simultaneously on the same plant.

123. Foxglove

- **Common name :** Foxglove, Common Foxglove, Purple Foxglove
- **Scientific name :** *Digitalis purpurea*
- **Family :** Plantaginaceae
- **Native land :** Temperate Europe

It is a herbaceous biennial or short-lived perennial plant. The name foxglove is derived from the shape of the flowers, which resemble the fingers of a glove. The plant grows up to 2-5 feet tall and unbranched. The leaves are soft, hairy, toothed, and lance-to-egg-shaped. The flowers are very showy, purple with purple mottling on the inside, and borne on a spike. It is a popular garden plant in southeast Alaska. Though considered highly poisonous yet this plant is the source of the cardiac drug digitalin.

124. Frog's Bit

- **Common name :** European Frog-bit
- **Scientific name :** *Hydrocharis morsus-ranae*
- **Family :** Hydrocharitaceae
- **Native land :** Europe and parts of Asia and Africa

European frog-bit is an annual herbaceous free-floating aquatic plant. Frog-bit is fast growing and spreads rapidly by stolons. It has no roots attached to the bed of the water body, but in situations where the vegetation is dense enough, the leaves may become emergent. By mid-summer, thick mats of interlocking plants can cover the surface of the water. European frog-bit greatly resembles miniature water lilies. It is considered a pest in various regions, as it colonises waterways and forms dense masses of vegetation on the surface, threatening native biodiversity.

125. Garland Chrysanthemum

- **Common name :** Garland Chrysanthemum, Crown Daisy
- **Scientific name :** *Glebionis coronaria*
- **Family :** Asteraceae
- **Native land :** Europe and Northern Asia

Garland chrysanthemum is a flowering annual plant. The plants are used as vegetables. They are about 12 inches tall. The leaves have the familiar chrysanthemum-like lobes. They are succulent with a strong aromatic and minty flavour. The ray flowers are yellow, single-petalled, and daisy-like. According to the sizes of the leaves and the depth of the leaf cut, there are large, medium and small leaf varieties. It can also be used for ornamental purposes in flower beds and borders. The plant is rich in vitamin B and mineral salts.

126. Garlic

- **Common name :** Garlic, Poor Man's Treacle
- **Scientific name :** *Allium sativum*
- **Family :** Amaryllidaceae
- **Native land :** Mediterranean area

Garlic is typically grown as an annual herb and vegetable. Its segmented bulbs are commonly used in cooking. The foliage consists of aromatic, linear, flattened, grass-like green leaves. The bulb is of a compound nature, consisting of numerous bulblets, known technically as cloves. In some varieties, a central scape topped by an umbel of pinkish-white flowers rises from each clump of leaves to 18 inches tall in summer. Garlic is widely used around the world for its pungent flavour as a seasoning or condiment. Garlic has been used as both food and medicine for thousands of years.

127. Golden Chain

- **Common name** : Golden Chain, Golden Rain
- **Scientific name** : *Laburnum anagyroides*
- **Family** : Fabaceae
- **Native land** : Southern Europe from France to the Balkan Peninsula

Golden chain is a large, robust, spreading deciduous flowering tree with glorious, golden-yellow spring colour every year. It grows up to 5-25 feet tall. It is quick-growing and looks spectacular even when not in bloom because of its pretty, cut foliage. The flowers are produced in long streams, and are fragrant. The wood is hard and heavy, of a yellow/brown colour. This type of wood is ideal for making posts, for woodturning and as fuel.

128. Good King Henry

- **Common name** : Poor-man's Asparagus
- **Scientific name** : *Blitum bonus-henricus*
- **Family** : Amaranthaceae/Chenopodiaceae
- **Native land** : Central and Southern Europe

Good King Henry is an annual or perennial plant. It is a dark-green, succulent plant, which grows up to 2 feet. The leaves are broad, triangular to diamond-shaped, with a pair of broad pointed lobes near the base. The flowers are green in colour. Each flower has five sepals. The seeds are reddish-green, 2-3 mm diameter. The plant grows abundantly in waste places near villages, having formerly been cultivated as a garden pot-herb. The fruit is bladder-like, containing a single seed. It is an easy-to-grow herb and is rich in iron and vitamin C.

129. Heart of Jesus

- **Common name** : Angel Wings, Elephant Ear
- **Scientific name** : *Caladium bicolor*
- **Family** : Araceae
- **Native land** : Northern South America

Caladiums are tuber-rooted tropical flowering perennials. They have no stems. Arrowhead-shaped leaves are of various shades, ranging from green mottled and blotched with pink, red, white or combinations thereof often with distinctively coloured veins. The plant grows up to 2 feet tall and up to 2 feet wide. Caladiums are used in shady beds and borders. They provide warm colour in areas too shady for most flowers. This plant often grown as a houseplant and tubers can be overwintered indoors. It can also be grown as an ornamental plant.

130. Honeysuckle

- **Common name :** Pink Honeysuckle, California Honeysuckle
- **Scientific name :** *Lonicera hispidula*
- **Family :** Caprifoliaceae
- **Native land :** California west coast of the United States

Pink honeysuckle is a perennial vine shrub. It is a low-elevation woodlands shrub. It has distinctive leaves growing opposite on the stems, the uppermost pairs fuses at the bases to surround the stem. Attractive pink honeysuckle blossoms at the end of the stem. It bears spherical red fruits which are edible but bitter. The stems are hollow and sturdy, and are used by the Pomo people as smoking pipes. The plant is drought-tolerant. The flowers attract hummingbirds; other birds eat the fruits.

131. Horseradish

- **Common name :** Horseradish
- **Scientific name :** *Armoracia rusticana*
- **Family :** Brassicaceae
- **Native land :** South-Eastern Europe and Western Asia

Horseradish is a herbaceous perennial plant. It is a somewhat coarse vegetable that is grown for its pungent, fleshy roots. It has large, variably sized, dock-like, toothed, shiny, dark green leaves. It has insignificant, whitish flowers which appear in summer. The leaves are textured like puckered crepe paper. In temperate Eastern Europe, it is indigenous. It has been used for medicinal and culinary purposes. In the past, physicians and healers used to recommend horseradish for everything from a sore throat to digestive upset.

132. Hosta

- **Common name :** Hosta, Blue Angle, Devil's Advocate
- **Scientific name :** *Hosta bressingham blue*
- **Family :** Asparagaceae
- **Native land :** North-East Asia (China, Japan, Korea, and the Russian Far East)

Hosta is a herbaceous perennial plant. It grows from rhizomes or stolons with broad lanceolate or ovate leaves. The leaves have wide variations in size by species. The enormous blue green leaves have streaky, wide green margins that lighten as the season progresses. White flowers appear in mid-summer. Its large leaves provide excellent coverage for dying bulb foliage. Light lavender flowers top the clump in midsummer.

133. Hyacinth

- **Common name :** Hyacinth, Garden Hyacinth, Dutch Hyacinth
- **Scientific name :** *Hyacinthus orientalis*
- **Family :** Asparagaceae
- **Native land :** Central and Southern Turkey, North-Western Syria, Lebanon

Hyacinth is a herbaceous perennial flowering plant. It is a spring flowering bulb that produces the spikes of flowers noted for their intense, often overpowering, fragrance. It typically grows 6-10 inches tall. Each bulb sends up 3-4 strap-shaped green leaves in early spring and a stiff densely flowered spike of extremely fragrant tubular flowers. Flower colours are in various shades of blue, purple, pink, red and white. Hyacinth is produced in group or mass in beds, borders, rock gardens, along walks. This species effectively mixes with other spring flowering bulbs.

134. Hydrangea

- **Common name :** Bigleaf Hydrangea
- **Scientific name :** *Hydrangea macrophylla*
- **Family :** Hydrangeaceae
- **Native land :** China, Japan and parts of Russia

Bigleaf hydrangea is a deciduous shrub. It is a very popular flowering shrub. The flowers are mostly produced in June and July but newer cultivars (that flower on new growth) flower through the summer. Depending on the particular cultivar, this plant bears one of two types of flowers. Plants with large globe-shaped flowers are called mopheads. Plants with flat flower clusters are called lacecaps; lacecaps are composed of a ring of showy large sterile florets on the outside and the centre is composed of less showy fertile flowers. They are produced in group or mass in the shrub border.

135. Hypericum

- **Common name :** Aaron's Beard, St. John's Wort
- **Scientific name :** *Hypericum calycinum*
- **Family :** Hypericaceae
- **Native land :** Southern Europe, South-Western Asia

Hypericum is an evergreen shrub. It is a stoloniferous sub-shrub. It grows up to 1 feet tall. It is a fast growing plant. It has large, rose-like, five-petaled, yellow flowers (with five petals) having numerous, bushy stamens with reddish anthers. The flowers appear singly or in groups of 2-3 and cover the plant in summer. Oval to oblong, distinctively net-veined leaves are rich green in the sun but are a lighter, yellowish green in shade. The plant is used to control erosion on slopes, or to cover the bare ground under the big oak tree.

136. Hyssop

- **Common name :** Hyssop
- **Scientific name :** *Hyssopus officinalis*
- **Family :** Lamiaceae
- **Native land :** Southern Europe eastward to Central Asia

Hyssop is a small herbaceous or semi-woody perennial plant. It grows up to 1.5 feet tall. It has slim, woody quadrangular stems and narrow, elliptical, dotted leaves that grow in pairs on the stem. It has long, leafy, half-whorled spikes of little flowers coloured violet-blue, pink, red, or white. The flowers blossom from June to September. In the European Middle Ages, hyssop was a stewing herb. Its modern uses are for flavouring meats, fish, vegetables, salads, sweets, and liquors. Honey made from hyssop pollen is very delicious. Hyssop oil extracted from the leaves is used as fragrance in soaps and cosmetics.

137. Ivy

- **Common name :** Ivy, Canarian Ivy, Algerian Ivy
- **Scientific name :** *Hedera canariensis*
- **Family :** Araliacea
- **Native land :** Canary Islands, Portugal, the Azores, and North Africa

Ivy is an evergreen perennial climbing or trailing woody shrub or bush. Its beautiful thick, leathery foliage seems a little shinier than English ivy. The leaves are broad, glossy dark green in colour and a little leathery, with 1-5 lobes, regular in size and shape. It is cultivated in gardens and used in floral arrangements. The flowers are greenish and the fruits are globular and black when ripe. It is widely cultivated in tropical and subtropical climates. Old vines can become quite woody.

138. Jack-in-the-Pulpit

- **Common name :** Dragon Root, Wild Turnip
- **Scientific name :** *Arisaema triphyllum*
- **Family :** Araceae
- **Native land :** Eastern and Mid-Western North America

It is a herbaceous perennial flower, spring-flowering bulb. It produces one to two 3-lobed leaves 12 to 18 inches high. The flowers have two distinct parts: a spathe, and a spadix. The spathe is petal-like and forms an upright 'hood'. The spadix is an erect, fleshy spike that is partially enclosed by the spadix. The plant bears ornamental fruit. In the fresh state, it is a violent irritant to the mucous membrane and when chewed it causes burning of the mouth and throat. If taken internally, this plant causes violent gastroenteritis which may end in death.

139. Japanese Wineberry

- **Common name :** Wineberry, Wine Raspberry, Japanese Wineberry
- **Scientific name :** *Rubus phoenicolasius*
- **Family :** Rosaceae
- **Native land :** Japan, Korea and China

It is a perennial shrub with long arching stems up to 9 feet in length. Upright stems have red gland tipped hair and small spines. The leaves are alternate, palmately compound, with 3 heart-shaped serrated leaflets. Small greenish flowers with white petals and reddish hair occur in late spring to early summer. The very edible raspberry-like fruit has bright red to orange-red colour, multiple drupes, and ripens in mid summer. Wineberries are juicy and very sour. They are a good source of vitamin C, antioxidants, minerals and fibre.

140. Jerusalem Sage

- **Common name :** Jerusalem Sage
- **Scientific name :** *Phlomis fruticosa*
- **Family :** Lamiaceae
- **Native land :** Mediterranean region

This plant can be herbaceous perennials or evergreen shrubs, with sage-like leaves and whorls of tubular, hooded flowers. They bloom around the months of March and June. The erect shoots bear grey-green ovate leaves. Foliage is silver in colour. Its height ranges from 60-120 cm. The plant can be used as a herb in cooking or brewed into tea. It tends to have a very strong flavour, so one or two leaves in a cup of boiling water or tea are usually sufficient.

141. Kachampuli

- **Common name :** Brindleberry, Malabar Tamarind
- **Scientific name :** *Garcinia gummi-gutta*
- **Family :** Clusiaceae
- **Native land :** Indonesia

This plant is an evergreen, dioecious, understorey tree. Its branching is usually horizontal or drooping with thick, glossy, dark green leaves. It is mainly grown for its fruit that looks like a small pumpkin and is green to pale yellow in colour. The fruit has a thin skin and deep vertical lobes. The size of the fruit varies from about the size of an orange to that of a grapefruit. The colour can vary considerably. When the rinds are dried and cured in preparation for storage and extraction, they are dark brown or black in colour. It is mostly used in cooking and also used commercially in curing fish, especially in Sri Lanka and South India.

142. Kiwifruit

- **Common name :** Kiwi, Chinese Gooseberry
- **Scientific name :** *Actinidia deliciosa*
- **Family :** Actinideaceae
- **Native land :** Southern China

Kiwi is a woody deciduous vine. It can grow up to 10 metres tall. The flowers are white to cream-coloured. The russet-brown fruit is an oval berry densely covered with short, stiff, brown hair. The fruit has green flesh containing many hundreds of tiny black seeds. The fruit has a tangy sweet flavour somewhat like a strawberry blended with a pineapple. This plant with its large heart-shaped leaves can spread to 30 feet wide. Kiwis contain around 10% total sugars. They are rich in vitamin C.

143. Kohlrabi

- **Common name :** German Turnip, Turnip Cabbage
- **Scientific name :** *Brassica oleracea var. gongylodes*
- **Family :** Brassicaceae/Cruciferae
- **Native land :** Europe and North Africa

Kohlrabi is an annual vegetable. It is a low, stout cultivar of cabbage. Kohlrabi is a strange looking vegetable, very different from other family members (cabbage, broccoli, etc). It is grown for its enlarged bulb-like swelling that develops on the stem a few inches above the ground. The plant resembles that of the cabbage by corm sprout long petioles (leaf stems) with leaves. The whole plant is less than 2 ft (0.6 metre) tall. It is a fast-growing plant that can be eaten raw as well as cooked.

144. Konjac

- **Common name :** Konjac
- **Scientific name :** *Amorphophallus konjac*
- **Family :** Araceae
- **Native land :** Warm sub-tropical to tropical Eastern Asia

Konjac is a perennial plant. It grows from a large corm up to 25 cm in diameter. It has a single leaf of about 1.3 metres in length, across, bipinnate, and divided into numerous leaflets. The flowers are produced on a spathe (a leaflike bract that encloses or subtends a flower cluster) enclosed by a dark purple spadix (a fleshy club-like spike bearing minute flowers). Flowering occurs in early spring if the corm is mature. The plant has long been used in China, Japan and South-East Asia as a food source and as a traditional medicine.

145. Lamb's Ear

- **Common name** : Lamb's Ears
- **Scientific name** : *Stachys byzantina*
- **Family** : Lamiaceae
- **Native land** : Central-Eastern Turkey, Northern Iran, Caucasus

Lamb's ear is a hardy herbaceous perennial. The shape of the leaf and texture resemble a lamb's ear. It is popular for its thick, soft, velvety, silver-grey leaves. The leaves are evergreen in warm climates, but will depreciate considerably in harsh winters. Small-leaved flowering stems with terminal spikes of insignificant, tiny, purplish-pink flowers appear in summer rising above the foliage to 10-15 inches tall. Once established, the plants are reasonably drought-tolerant, making this a good choice for a dry sunny border or gravel garden.

146. Laurus

- **Common name** : Bay
- **Scientific name** : *Laurus nobilis*
- **Family** : Lauraceae
- **Native land** : Mediterranean

Bay is an evergreen tree. It may grow to 40 feet in its native regions. The tree or woody potted shrub bears dense, pointed, elliptical leaves, rather leathery in texture. The leaves are bright green when young and darker green when they mature. The leaves may have smooth or crenate margins. The aroma of the leaves is not free; the leaves have to be rubbed to release it. In warm areas, bays bear yellowish-white fluffy flowers and small black fruit. Pot-grown bays seldom produce flower and fruit. The other species called Mountain laurel (*Kalmia latifolia*) is a poisonous species to humans and most other animals.

147. Lavender

- **Common name** : Lavender
- **Scientific name** : *Lavandula angustifolia*
- **Family** : Lamiaceae
- **Native land** : Western Mediterranean

Lavender is a herbaceous perennial. This is a semi-woody plant that typically grows to 1.5-3.0 feet. It has narrow, grey-green leaves on square stems. Purple flowers appear in terminal spikes in late spring to early summer. Both foliage and flowers are highly aromatic. Leaves are evergreen in warm winter climates. Lavender flowers and grey-green leaves provide mid-summer colour and contrast to herb garden or scented garden. Lavender flowers and foliage are also popular additions to sachets and potpourris. Lavender flower oils are used in cosmetic industry.

148. Leek

- **Common name** : Wild Leek
- **Scientific name** : *Allium ampeloprasum*
- **Family** : Alliaceae
- **Native land** : Eastern Mediterranean lands and the Middle East

Leek is a hardy, vigorous, biennial plant. Leek has been known and used for centuries for its medicinal properties, although nowadays it is used mainly as food or flavour. In the first season of its growth, long linear leaves arise from a compressed stem or stem plate; the thick leaf bases overlap and are arranged concentrically in a nearly cylindrical bulb. A tuft of fibrous, shallow roots grows from the base of the stem plate. The edible parts of the leek plant are the light green stalk (or stem) and its white bulb.

149. Lemon Balm

- **Common name** : Lemon Balm, Balm Mint
- **Scientific name** : *Melissa officinalis*
- **Family** : Lamiaceae
- **Native land** : Southern Europe, Eastern, Mid-Western and Pacific North-West states

Lemon balm is a bushy herbaceous perennial of the mint family. The leaves are wrinkled, ovate, medium and green. Tiny, two-lipped, white flowers appear in the leaf axils throughout summer. The leaves are edible and may be added to salads, soups, sauces or vegetables and are also used to flavour teas. The plant also has a history of herbal medicine usage for a variety of purposes. It is typically grown in herb gardens and border fronts for its lemon-scented leaves.

150. Lemon

- **Common name** : Lemon Verbena, Lemon Beebrush
- **Scientific name** : *Aloysia citriodora*
- **Family** : Verbenaceae
- **Native land** : Argentina, Chile

Lemon verbena is a herbaceous perennial woody shrub. It produces shiny lanceolate green leaves that have a strong aroma (without crushing) and taste of lemon. The plants grow up to 10-15 feet tall in the tropics, but in containers it grows only 2-4 feet tall. It is sensitive to cold, losing leaves at temperatures below 0°C. The leaves are strongest at the time of flowering. The leaves and the flowers are used for culinary purposes (teas, desserts, fruit salads and jams), for perfumes and cosmetics, for potpourris and as herbal medicines (colds, fevers, dyspepsia and diarrhoea).

151. Lettuce

- **Common name** : Lettuce
- **Scientific name** : *Lactuca sativa*
- **Family** : Asteraceae
- **Native land** : Mediterranean Regions to Siberia

Lettuce is an annual glabrous herb with a thin taproot and an erect stem 30-100 cm tall, branched in the upper part. The leaves are spirally arranged, forming a dense rosette. It grows in a basal rosette at first, then either in a loose or a tightly rolled head, and eventually along an upright stem that supports the flowers. Lettuce is almost exclusively used as a fresh vegetable in salads, but some forms are also cooked. Many of the red and purple lettuces make excellent borders around cool season flower beds.

152. Lotus Roots

- **Common name** : Sacred Lotus
- **Scientific name** : *Nelumbo nucifera*
- **Family** : Nelumbonaceae
- **Native land** : Asia (Iran to Japan), Northern Australia

Sacred lotus is an aquatic, herbaceous perennial plant. It is a large-flowered lotus. It grows up to 3-6 feet tall in shallow water and spreads by thickened rhizomes rooted in the mud. It has rounded, parasol-like, upward-cupped, waxy green leaves. The flower blooms for about three days, opening in the morning and closing at night each day. Receptacles acquire a woody texture when dried and are highly prized for dried flower arrangements. The rhizomes, leaves and seeds of lotus are edible and are sometimes used in Asian cooking.

153. Mint

- **Common name** : Mint
- **Scientific name** : *Mentha longifolia*
- **Family** : Lamiaceae
- **Native land** : Europe, Asia, and Australia

It is a very variable herbaceous perennial plant. It has square stems, opposite, aromatic leaves, and small flowers usually of a pale purple, pink, or white colour arranged in clusters, either forming separate whorls or crowded together in a terminal spike. Many species are used as flavourings for foods, but, in cookery, the term mint usually refers to peppermint or spearmint. Oils of mints are used as scents in perfumery and as flavouring in candy, liqueur, gum, dentifrices and medicines.

154. Miracle Leaf

- **Common name** : Miracle Leaf, Air Plant
- **Scientific name** : *Bryophyllum pinnatum*
- **Family** : Crassulaceae
- **Native land** : Madagascar

Miracle leaf is a succulent perennial herb, growing widely and used in folklore medicine in tropical Africa, tropical America, India, China and Australia. Its stem is hollow, four-angled and usually branched. The leaves are opposite, decussate and succulent. The lower leaves are simple, whereas the upper ones are foliate and long-petioled. They are fleshy dark green that are distinctively scalloped and trimmed in red. It is astringent, sour in taste, sweet in the post-digestive effect and has hot potency. It is well known for its haemostatic and wound-healing properties.

155. Mistletoe

- **Common name** : Mistletoe
- **Scientific name** : *Viscum album*
- **Family** : Santalaceae
- **Native land** : Europe and Western and Southern Asia

It is a hemi-parasitic shrub, that grows on the stems of other trees. This partially parasitic species is well known for its waxy white berries and in Europe is strongly associated with Christmas. It is highly sought-after for use as a winter decoration. The leathery textured, strap-shaped leaves in opposite pairs are a yellowish-green in colour. Mistletoe leaves, stems and berries can be poisonous to humans if ingested, and pets such as dogs are also at risk when mistletoe is brought indoors.

156. Monarda

- **Common name** : Red Beebalm
- **Scientific name** : *Monarda didyma*
- **Family** : Lamiaceae
- **Native land** : North America

Beebalm is a herbaceous perennial flower. The species with purple-green rosette buds show colour early in spring and grow into large red tubular flowers. Other varieties come in white and shades of pink, purple and blue. It is valued in ornamental plantings for its scarlet blooms that attract bees, hummingbirds and insects. Fresh flowers are used as a garnishing agent for green salads, fruit salads, cakes or preserves. The aromatic leaves serve as a substitute for mint and can be dried for tea. Dried leaves and flowers are also useful in sachets and potpourris.

157. Morning Glory

- **Common name** : Morning Glory, Japanese Morning Glory
- **Scientific name** : *Ipomoea nil*
- **Family** : Convolvulacea
- **Native land** : California

Morning glory is a climbing annual flowering herb or vine. Its leaves are broadly ovate or nearly circular, base heart-shaped, margin entire or 3-lobed. Its stem is clothed by long hair. Its flowers are solitary, axillary, funnel-shaped, bluish or purplish. The flowers are several centimetres wide and appear in various shades of blue, pink or rose, often with white stripes or edges or blends of colours. It is cultivated as an attractive ornamental plant in many places.

158. Mother-of-millions

- **Common name** : Mother-of-millions, Chandelier Plant
- **Scientific name** : *Bryophyllum delagoense*
- **Family** : Crassulaceae
- **Native land** : Africa and Madagascar

Mother-of-millions is a succulent perennial plant. It reproduces rapidly, producing hundreds of tiny plantlets which quickly form new colonies. It is adapted to dry conditions and can survive long periods of drought. The plant flowers from May to October. Mother-of-millions is toxic when ingested by livestock; it is also poisonous to humans and household pets. The plant is an escaped ornamental plant.

159. Mullein

- **Common name** : Great Mullein
- **Scientific name** : *Verbascum thapsus*
- **Family** : Scrophulariaceae
- **Native land** : Europe and in temperate Asia, and North America

Mullein is a hairy biennial plant. It is a common weedy plant that spreads by prolifically producing seeds. Its small yellow flowers are densely grouped on a tall stem, which grows from a large rosette of leaves. It also hosts many insects, some of which can be harmful to other plants. Although insects are easy to remove by hand yet their populations are difficult to eliminate permanently. It is widely used for herbal remedies, with well-established emollient and astringent properties. The plant has also been used to make dyes and torches.

160. Mustard Green

- **Common name** : Mustard Green
- **Scientific name** : *Brassica juncea*
- **Family** : Brassicaceae
- **Native land** : Russia to Central Asia

Mustard green is an annual, cruciferous vegetable. Mustard green has pale green foliage, with some hair on the first leaves. The lower leaves are deeply lobed, while the upper leaves are narrow and entire. The flowers are pale yellow and open progressively upwards from the base of the raceme. Seeds are round and can be yellow or brown. The leaves, the seeds, and the stem of this mustard variety are edible.

161. Nasturtium

- **Common name** : Nasturtium, Monks Cress
- **Scientific name** : *Tropaeolum majus*
- **Family** : Tropaeolaceae
- **Native land** : South America

Nasturtium is an annual and perennial herbaceous flowering plant. This variety includes climbing, dwarf, and bushy types. The stems and leafstalks are pale green in colour, hairless and somewhat fleshy. The green or slightly bluish-green leaves are borne on stalks. These leaves are rounded in shape with entire, undulate, or slightly lobed margins. The leaves are hairless and have several prominent veins that radiate outwards from the centre of the leaf blade. All parts of this plant are edible. Nasturtiums have been used in herbal medicine for their antiseptic and expectorant qualities.

162. Nightshade

- **Common name** : Bitter Nightshade, Violet Bloom
- **Scientific name** : *Solanum dulcamara*
- **Family** : Solanaceae
- **Native land** : Europe and Asia

Bitter nightshade is a perennial climbing or trailing vine. It reproduces by seeds and rooting at the nodes of the prostrate stems. The plant has two leaf forms that, along with its blue-violet flowers and bright red berries, can be useful to distinguish bitter nightshade from the other nightshade species. Young stems and leaves are generally hairy. The flowers appear in branched, drooping clusters that attach to the main stem opposite the leaves. The fruits are oval, thin-skinned, juicy, bright red berries. The leaves are considered moderately poisonous if ingested.

163. Nodding Wild Onion

- **Common name :** Nodding Onion, Lady's Leek
- **Scientific name :** *Allium cernuum*
- **Family :** Amaryllidaceae
- **Native land :** Canada to Mexico

Nodding onion is a perennial plant. It consists of a tuft of basal leaves from which one or more flowering stalks emerge. The leaves are grass-like, wide, keeled along the mid-rib and sheathing the stem near the soil line, appearing to be basal. The central flowering stem, which rises above the leaves, is stiff and smooth. All parts of this plant have an onion-like smell when cut or bruised. Although the bulbs and the leaves of this plant were once used in cooking (stews) or eaten raw yet nodding onion is not generally considered to be of culinary value today.

164. Onion

- **Common name :** Onion
- **Scientific name :** *Allium cepa*
- **Family :** Amaryllidaceae/Alliaceae
- **Native land :** South-Western Asia

An onion is a herbaceous biennial plant. It is grown throughout the world, chiefly in the temperate zones. Most members of this family have an underground storage system, such as a bulb or tuber. The onion has one or more leafless flower stalks that reach a height of 2.5-6.0 feet. Flower stalks terminate in a cluster of small greenish white flowers. The leaf bases of the developing plant swell to form the underground bulb that is the mature, edible onion. Most commercially cultivated onions are grown from the small black seeds. Onions are among the hardiest of all garden vegetable plants.

165. Oregano

- **Common name :** Oregano
- **Scientific name :** *Origanum vulgare subsp. gracile*
- **Family :** Lamiaceae
- **Native land :** Kyrgyzstan

Oregano is a perennial herb. It is a bushy, semi-woody, sub-shrub with upright or spreading stems and branches. The aromatic leaves are oval-shaped. The leaves may be clipped fresh as needed or dried for year-round use. Best leaf flavour usually occurs just prior to flowering, but the quality of flavour can vary considerably from plant to plant. Tiny, white to rosy pink flowers appear in loose, terminal or axillary spikes throughout summer. Aromatic dark green leaves are commonly used in cooking as a seasoning. Dried oregano has a stronger flavour.

166. Palm Lily

- **Common name** : Cabbage Palm, Cabbage Tree, New Zealand Cabbage Palm, Red Grass Palm
- **Scientific name** : *Cordyline australis*
- **Family** : Asparagaceae
- **Native land** : New Zealand (Australasia), Morocco

This is a palm-like, sub-tropical tree. The plant has several stout branches arising from a single trunk. The leaves are long, sword-shaped, in dense clusters at the branch tips. The plant bears large panicles of small, fragrant cream flowers. The bloom time is in spring. Vast spikes of scented flowers in late summer can fill a garden with perfume. Resultant seed-laden trusses help birds through winter. It is primarily the combination of its tall slender trunk and the explosions of strap-like foliage at the top of the trunk that gives it its palm-like image.

167. Pea

- **Common name** : Garden Pea
- **Scientific name** : *Pisum sativum*
- **Family** : Fabaceae
- **Native land** : South-West Asia, Southern Europe and North-East Africa

Garden pea is a glabrous, hardy, annual, climbing leguminous plant. It has a non-edible fibrous pod that bore edible round seeds. The seeds are a highly nutritious food, having a high protein and fibre-content. Its stems are roundish and hollow that are covered with a waxy bloom. The leaves consist of one or more pairs of opposite leaflets. The young tips, called pea shoots, may be harvested and cooked as a pot herb. Pea shoots are a delicacy in Chinese cuisine.

168. Peony

- **Common name** : Peony
- **Scientific name** : *Paeonia caucasica*
- **Family** : Paeoniaceae
- **Native land** : Caucasus

Peony is a deciduous, woody shrub. It is a taprooted plant with thick horizontal rhizome and leafy stems. The leaves have elongate-ovate or elongate-elliptical lobes with greyish wax and short sparse hair beneath. Its flowers are large and single. They are often bright crimson, sometimes pink. The light pink-rose petals of the large, semi-double flowers almost obscure the bushy centre clump of yellow stamens. Large rosy pink flowers with trembling golden thread-like anthers give way to three-horned fruits. The flowers bloom in early spring. The fruits then open to reveal red and purple blue seeds.

169. Pepper

- **Common name** : Bell Pepper, Capsicum, Sweet Pepper
- **Scientific name** : *Capsicum annuum*
- **Family** : Solanaceae
- **Native land** : Tropical North and South America

Capsicum or bell pepper is a herbaceous perennial plant. Plants of this species grow in shrubby mounds. The flowers are white or yellow and the leaves are green and lance-shaped to oval medium. The flowers give way to edible peppers, ranging from extremely hot chilli peppers to sweet bell peppers. Peppers are used fresh, cooked, or dried in an enormous variety of dishes characteristic of different regional cuisines. They are high in vitamins A and C. Some varieties have been developed to use as ornamentals.

170. Periwinkle

- **Common name** : Madagascar Periwinkle, Periwinkle
- **Scientific name** : *Catharanthus roseus*
- **Family** : Apocynaceae
- **Native land** : Madagascar

Periwinkle is an evergreen subshrub or herbaceous plant. It produces attractive bushy foliage that is covered by an often profuse bloom of phlox-like flowers from summer to frost. Much softwood branches from the ground and gives it an appearance of fullness. It blooms best in summers. The leaves are oval to oblong. Tubular flowers have five flattened petal-like lobes and appear singly in the upper leaf axils. The flowers come in a wide variety of colours. Some varieties are used as a traditional medicinal plant used to control diabetes, in various regions of the world.

171. Persimmon

- **Common name** : Asian Persimmon, Japanese Persimmon
- **Scientific name** : *Diospyros kaki*
- **Family** : Ebenaceae
- **Native land** : Asia (China, Japan)

Asian persimmon is a deciduous tree. This is an excellent fruit tree for ornamental use and makes an excellent specimen. The tree looks attractive when leaves have fallen in autumn, displaying the bright yellow-orange fruits throughout the canopy. It develops an attractive red autumn colour, but the two to four-inch-diameter fruits can be a big ness when they fall from the tree. The tree has good drought-tolerance. The fruit is a sweet, slightly tangy fruit with a soft to occasionally fibrous texture.

172. Phacelia

- **Common name** : Lacy Phacelia or Purple Tansy
- **Scientific name** : *Phacelia tanacetifolia*
- **Family** : Boraginaceae
- **Native land** : South-Western United States and Northern Mexico

Phacelia is a herbaceous, non-leguminous flowering plant. The foliage appears ferny, and the flowers are in flat-topped clusters in the shades of purple or occasionally white. Spring and summer-planted phacelia blooms approximately 6-8 weeks after germination. Phacelia is a long-day plant and requires a minimum of 13 hours of daylight to initiate flowering. It flowers from mid-April to early September. The flower is ideal as a cut flower and is loved by bees. It is an excellent source of attraction for lots of insects like lace-wings and ladybirds.

173. Pineapple Sage

- **Common name** : Pineapple Sage
- **Scientific name** : *Salvia elegans*
- **Family** : Lamiaceae
- **Native land** : Mexico, Guatemala

Pineapple sage is a perennial shrub. It has opposite, ovate, soft-hairy, light green leaves on square stems. The plant has pineapple aroma and flavour in its foliage when crushed. It produces slender trumpet-shaped red flowers. The red flowers are attractive to hummingbirds and butterflies. The leaves and the flowers of pineapple sage are edible. The flowers may be used as a garnish, or may be added to fruit cocktails or salads. The leaves may be added to salads or to hot/iced teas. The plant is extensively used for the treatment of anxiety, and also for lowering blood pressure.

174. Pointleaf Manzanita

- **Common name** : Pointleaf Manzanita, Mexican Manzanita
- **Scientific name** : *Arctostaphylos pungens*
- **Family** : Ericaceae
- **Native land** : Mexico

It is a perennial, evergreen plant. The leaves are green, stiff, leathery, held vertically, and have sharply pointed tips. The branches have beautiful, smooth, reddish-brown bark. The flowers are shaped like inverted vases and grow in clusters at the branch tips. The flowers are followed by round, reddish-brown to orange berries. Animals and birds eat the fruit. The fruit is edible either raw or cooked, but it is dry and mealy. The fruit is used to make jellies and is used as a diuretic.

175. Poison Hemlock

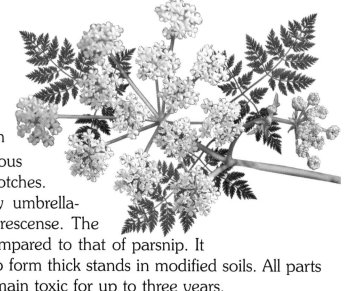

- **Common name** : Herb Bennet, Poison Hemlock, Poison Parsley
- **Scientific name** : *Conium maculatum*
- **Family** : Apiaceae (Umbelliferae)
- **Native land** : Europe and the Mediterranean region

Poison hemlock is a highly poisonous perennial herbaceous flowering plant. It has hairless hollow stalks with purple blotches. The leaves are triangular in shape. It produces many umbrella-shaped flower clusters in an open and branching inflorescense. The leaves and the root emit an unpleasant odour often compared to that of parsnip. It produces a large number of seeds that allow the plant to form thick stands in modified soils. All parts of the plant are poisonous and even the dead canes remain toxic for up to three years.

176. Poppy

- **Common name** : Opium Poppy
- **Scientific name** : *Papaver somniferum*
- **Family** : Papaveraceae
- **Native land** : Mediterranean Basin, South-Eastern Europe, and Western Asia

Poppies are herbaceous annual, biennial or short-lived perennial plants. They have brilliant white or red flowers, growing on central bulbous pods. When scratched, the pod produces milky latex called opium. This latex contains a variety of opiates, including codeine and morphine. The seeds themselves contain very small amounts of opiates. Poppy seeds of *Papaver somniferum* are an important food-item and the source of poppy seed oil, healthy edible oil, that have many uses.

177. Potato

- **Common name** : Potato
- **Scientific name** : *Solanum tuberosum*
- **Family** : Solanaceae
- **Native land** : South America

The potato is a starchy, tuberous perennial crop. It is widely cultivated for its edible tubers, which are used to produce a variety of products including chips, crisps and vodka. It is considered to be the fourth most important food-crop (after wheat, maize and rice) across the world. Potato plant leaves are compound. The tubers are not roots, but modified stems or rhizomes, and the 'eyes' are leaf buds. Potato flowers are rather showy; they are star-shaped, white, lavender, pink or light blue with yellow centres. The fruits are like small green tomatoes, about an inch in diameter, and contain hundreds of seeds.

178. Pumpkin

- **Common name** : Pumpkin
- **Scientific name** : *Cucurbita pepo*
- **Family** : Cucurbitaceae
- **Native land** : North America

Pumpkin is an annual climber. It grows up to 2 feet. The plant blooms from July to September, and the seeds ripen from August to October. The fruit is round, with a smooth, slightly ribbed skin and deep yellow to orange colouration. The thick shell contains the seeds and the pulp. The plant is self-fertile. The plant has been cultivated for its edible fruits for thousands of years and remains a crop plant of great economic importance today. There are also several varieties of inedible gourds exhibiting terrific range in shapes, colours, texture and sizes.

179. Radicchio

- **Common name** : Red chicory
- **Scientific name** : *Cichorium intybus*
- **Family** : Asteraceae
- **Native land** : Europe

Chicory is a tender perennial grown as an annual plant. It is sometimes known as Italian chicory. It is a woody plant. Chicory has long, deep taproot that is milky inside. Radicchio leaves are stalked, hairy, lanceolate and large, coarsely toothed, growing in clustered formation from plant base in spreading rosette while the upper leaves are small. The small red and white heads of this chicory family member form best in cool weather. It is a staple vegetable in Italian salads with its bright colour and bitter taste but not overpowering flavour. It is a nutritious vegetable.

180. Radish

- **Common name** : Radish
- **Scientific name** : *Raphanus sativus*
- **Family** : Brassicaceae
- **Native land** : Europe and the UK

Radish is an edible root vegetable. It is an extremely variable species of a garden vegetable. Some are annuals while some biennials. Radish leaves usually are medium green and lobed, and have a rough texture, but some are purplish and some are smooth. The flowers are white, pink or purple. Most types are grown for their enlarged roots. The seed pods are sickle-shaped. They are full of little round seeds. Some are small 'salad radishes' with red skins or pure white throughout.

181. Red Clover

- **Common name** : Red Clover
- **Scientific name** : *Trifolium pratense*
- **Family** : Fabaceae
- **Native land** : Europe, Western Asia and North-West Africa

Red clover is a biennial or short-lived perennial. It grows up to 3 feet tall. The plant grows as one of two types: medium (double-cut) or mammoth (single-cut). The plant has hollow, hairy stems and branches. The taproot of red clover is extensively branched. The flowers are borne in compact clusters or heads and are usually rose-pink in colour. The seed pods are small, short, and contain kidney-shaped seeds that vary in colour from yellow to deep violet. Red clover is primarily used for hay, pasture, silage and soil improvement. Red clover is commonly used to make a sweet-tasting herbal tea.

182. Red Deadnettle

- **Common name** : Red Dead Nettle
- **Scientific name** : *Lamium purpureum*
- **Family** : Lamiaceae
- **Native land** : Europe

Red deadnettle may grow as an annual or a biennial. It is a hairy plant that branches from the base. The leaves often have a purple-grey tinge to them. The upper-most leaves can become deep purple-red when the plant grows in areas where it is more exposed to strong sunlight. The plant blooms from March to October, and the flowers are pink-purple in colour. The flowers and the leaves are concentrated towards the top of the stem. Young plants have edible tops and leaves that are used in salads or used as spring vegetables.

183. Red Goosefoot

- **Common name** : Red Goosefoot, Coastblite Goosefoot
- **Scientific name** : *Oxybasis rubra*
- **Family** : Chenopodiaceae
- **Native land** : North America and Eurasia

Red goosefoot is an annual flowering plant. The plant grows up to 3 feet tall. It is often tinged with red all over. Besides the stem, even the vegetative leaves are sometimes red. The leaves are oval or triangle-shaped, and have toothed appearance. The small petal-less flowers are in dense spikes. It blooms from August to October. The seeds are dark red-brown. The stems are ridged and green to red. Red goosefoot is a favourite food of birds and is also good for poultry.

184. Rhododendron

- **Common name** : Alpine Rose
- **Scientific name** : *Rhododendron ferrugineum*
- **Family** : Ericaceae
- **Native land** : Himalayas, from Kashmir eastwards to Nagaland

Rhododendron is either evergreen or deciduous, and found mainly in Asia. It also grows on the slopes of the Alps, so it is also called Alpine rose. It has broad, dark green leaves, with a silvery, fawn or brown hairy coating beneath. It blooms in late spring to early summer. Flower colours include pink, red, violet, yellow, and white, depending on species and variety. Its leaves are used shortly before blooming. The plant is generally considered to be anti-rheumatic, diuretic and diaphoretic. The flowers are used to make beverages like squashes and syrups.

185. Rosemary

- **Common name** : Rosemary
- **Scientific name** : *Rosmarinus officinalis*
- **Family** : Lamiaceae
- **Native land** : Mediterranean region

Rosemary is a woody, perennial herb. It is a generally erect, rounded, evergreen shrub with aromatic, needle-like, grey-green leaves and tiny, two-lipped, pale blue to white flowers. It grows up to 4-6 feet tall in areas where it is winter-hardy. Fresh or dried leaves may be used in a variety of cooking applications such as stews, breads, stuffings, herbal butters or vinegars. Its oil is commercially used in some perfumes, soaps, shampoos, lotions and other toiletries. Rosemary has been used for a variety of medicinal and curative purposes.

186. Rose

- **Common name** : Red rose
- **Scientific name** : *Rosa kordesii*
- **Family** : Rosaceae
- **Native land** : Europe, North America, and North-West Africa

Rosa kordesii is a deciduous shrub. It is also known as a climbing or pillar rose. It grows up to 8-10 feet tall. It can also be grown as a 4-6 feet tall free-standing shrub. The leaves are borne alternately on the stem. Foliage is glossy, dark green. The plant features profuse clusters of fragrant, crimson red, single flowers with white eyes. The plant blooms from late spring to frost. Roses are best known as ornamental plants grown for their flowers in the garden and sometimes indoors. They have been also used for commercial perfumery and commercial cut-flower crops.

187. Rutabaga

- **Common name** : Rutabaga, Oilseed Rape, Rapaseed
- **Scientific name** : *Brassica napus*
- **Family** : Brassicaceae
- **Native land** : Europe

Rutabaga is an annual plant. It has a long, usually thin taproot. Its leaves are smooth, bluish green, and deeply scalloped, and the bases of the upper leaves clasp the stem. It bears yellow flowers (with four petals) in spikes. Each round, elongated pod has a short beak and contains many seeds. These seeds yield oil, canola. Canola oil is treated for use in cooking, as an ingredient in soap and margarine, and as a lamp fuel (colza oil). The seeds are used as a bird's feed, and the seed residue after oil extraction is used as fodder.

188. Rye

- **Common name** : Rye
- **Scientific name** : *Secale cereale*
- **Family** : Poaceae
- **Native land** : Mediterranean region and Western Asia

Rye is one of the world's most important cultivated grains. It is sometimes a weed of grain crops such as wheat. It is also widely planted as a cover crop, and is sometimes used to prevent erosion. The plant has spikes composed of two or more spikelets bearing florets that develop one-seeded fruits, or grains. It is high in carbohydrates. Rye is used chiefly as flour for bread, as livestock feed, and as a pasture plant. Because of its dark colour, a loaf made entirely from rye flour is called black bread.

189. Sea Kale

- **Common name** : Sea Kale, Sea Cabbage
- **Scientific name** : *Crambe maritima*
- **Family** : Brassicaceae
- **Native land** : Europe, North Africa, South-West Asia

It is a robust herbaceous perennial that forms a clump of large, lobed, wavy-edged blue-green leaves. It grows mainly on seaside shingle and sandy beaches above the high tide line. The plant bears dense racemes of small white flowers in early summer. Honey-fragrant, clustered sprays of white, flowers (with four petals) rise from the basal leaves. From May to July, this plant bears large flat-topped clusters of white flowers. It is pollinated by many insects as it has fragrant aroma. Young or blanched leaves are cooked and eaten.

190. Sea Holly

- **Common name :** Variable-leaved Sea Holly
- **Scientific name :** *Eryngium variifolium*
- **Family :** Apiaceae
- **Native land :** North Africa

It is an evergreen perennial that forms a clump of rounded basal leaves with white veins. The stem is branched and leafy. It bears silvery-blue flower-heads with narrow, spiny silver bracts. The foliage is white, variegated, dark-green in summer. Foliage is evergreen in warm winter climates. Bloom time is June to August. The plant is compact enough to include in the rock garden, in the sunny border or in containers. Plants are very tolerant of hot, dry sites once established.

191. Silver Shield Sorrel

- **Common name :** French Sorrel, Buckler Sorrel
- **Scientific name :** *Rumex scutatus*
- **Family :** Polygonaceae
- **Native land :** South of France, Italy, Switzerland, Germany and Barbary

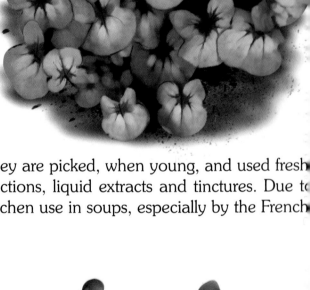

It is a mat-forming perennial. The whole plant is intensely glaucous. In areas of very mild winters, it produces leaves year-round. Red-green flowers appear in loose. The leaves are very succulent, fleshy and brittle. They are picked, when young, and used fresh. The roots are lifted in autumn and dried for use in decoctions, liquid extracts and tinctures. Due to the presence of acid in leaves, the plant is preferred for kitchen use in soups, especially by the French. The leaves also make good spring perennial salads.

192. Small Duckweed

- **Common name :** Small Duckweed
- **Scientific name :** *Lemna minor*
- **Family :** Araceae
- **Native land :** Africa, Asia, Europe and North America

Duckweeds are small, free-floating aquatic perennials that combine to form a green 'carpet' on the surface of the water. Each plant consists of a single, rounded, leaf-like body. It is the smallest flowering plant. Duckweed has no stems and no leaves. Some may have tiny roots. They grow best in nutrient-rich waters and are common in garden ponds. Duckweed does not flower frequently, and usually reproduces by budding on the margin or base of the 'fronds'. Duckweed is eaten by people in Thailand. It is used as a feed for fish (carp), poultry (chickens, ducks), livestock (pigs).

193. Sorrel (Garden)

- **Common name :** Garden Sorrel, Common Sorrel, Sour Dock
- **Scientific name :** *Rumex acetosa*
- **Family :** Polygonaceae
- **Native land :** North Temperate Arctic Regions

It is an erect perennial with edible, sour-tasting oblong leaves. The leaves are arrow-shaped at the base. Small reddish flowers appear in a narrow panicle or raceme. Plants form foliage clumps with three-foot-long leafy stems. Fresh young leaves are added to salads, sauces, soups, cream cheese and egg dishes, or pureed to add colour and acidity to mayonnaise. The juice is used to remove rust, mould, and ink stains from linen, wood, silver, and wicker. The deep roots of this herb may make it difficult to eradicate once it is well established.

194. Spatterdock

- **Common name :** Cow Lily, Yellow Pond Lily, Yellow Water Lily
- **Scientific name :** *Nuphar advena*
- **Family :** Nymphaeaceae
- **Native land :** North America

It is a perennial, herbaceous, emergent aquatic plant. The plant grows to the surface of the water from a thick horizontal root-stock. The stem is absent. The flowers grow on long peduncles and the leaves on separate petioles. The fruit is a depressed, globular, fleshy body and seeds are oblong, stipulates. The flowers open as the sun rises and close entirely during the mid-day heat and at night. Interestingly, when the flowers close in the evening, they sometimes trap beetles overnight, releasing them when they reopen the next morning. The starchy roots were eaten by Native-Americans, so were the seeds.

195. Spinach

- **Common name :** Spinach, Winter spinach
- **Scientific name :** *Spinacia oleracea*
- **Family :** Chenopodiaceae
- **Native land :** Asia, especially Afghanistan and Tajikistan

Spinach is an annual plant, long cultivated for the sake of its succulent leaves. It is an easy-to-grow, nutritious, cool-season crop. The leaves are somewhat triangular and may be flat or puckered. The edible leaves are arranged in a rosette, from which a seedstalk emerges. However, it is recommended to plant spinach early because it's quick to turn bitter and go to seed (bolt) as the weather warms and days lengthen. Spinach is shallow-rooted and requires consistent moisture to prevent bolting. It has high content of iron and vitamins A and C. Spinach is served as a green salad and as a cooked vegetable.

196. Spurge

- **Common name :** Cushion Spurge
- **Scientific name :** *Euphorbia epithymoides*
- **Family :** Euphorbiaceae
- **Native land :** Central and Southern Europe and to Asia Minor

It is a long-lived, drought-tolerant and non-spreading plant. It is a mounded clump-forming plant that is one of the best for borders. The plant bears dense, flattened yellow flowers in spring, and is one of the few perennials with showy autumn foliage. The leaves are medium to dark green, or tinged with purple or red. In autumn, they turn to a showy red, purple or orange. The showy yellow floral bracts provide the colour. However, the flowers are nondescript.

197. Squash

- **Common name :** Zucchini, Yellow Squash, Scalloped Squash, Patty Pan Squash
- **Scientific name :** *Cucurbita pepo*
- **Family :** Cucurbitaceae
- **Native land :** North, Central and South America

It is a tender easy-to-grow short-season annual. Most summer squash grow on compact vines, in contrast to the sprawling vines of most winter squash and pumpkins. The plant blooms from mid-summer to early autumn. Flowers are sometimes battered and fried or stuffed. These plants have separate male and female flowers on the same plant. The colour of the flower is yellow and foliage colour is medium green. The stems of these squash are deeply ridged. Squash is an excellent source of manganese and a very good source of vitamin C.

198. Summer Savory

- **Common name :** Summer Savory
- **Scientific name :** *Satureja hortensis*
- **Family :** Labiatae
- **Native land :** Mediterranean region, South-Eastern Europe

Summer savory is a hardy, pubescent annual, with slender erect stems. The plant blooms in spring to summer. It bears very small, pale lilac-pink flowers borne in widely spaced axillary whorls of 2 to 5 flower clusters. The leaves have a pungent spicy scent. It was (and is) used as a sauce seasoning that was poured over poultry, fish, and meat as well as used as an 'antiseptic' for the entire digestive tract. It has aromatic properties, and may be added to medicines for its aromatic and warming qualities.

199. Sweet Cicely

- **Common name :** British Myrrh, Garden Myrrh, Great Chervil, Myrrh
- **Scientific name :** *Myrrhis odorata*
- **Family :** Apiaceae
- **Native land :** Southern Europe

It is a tall, hardy perennial herb. The plant has bright green, 2- to 3-pinnate leaves and white flowers in umbels, followed by spindle-shaped fruits. The leaves are very large, somewhat downy beneath, and have a flavour rather like Anise. Sweet cicely is very attractive to bees; in the north of England it is said that the seeds are used to polish and scent oak floors and furniture. The plant is useful in coughs and flatulence. The fresh root may be eaten freely or used in infusion with brandy or water.

200. Sweet Pea

- **Common name :** Sweet Pea
- **Scientific name :** *Lathyrus odoratus*
- **Family :** Fabaceae
- **Native land :** Sicily, Southern Italy and the Aegean Islands

It is a popular annual flower whose flowering time ranges from late spring to summer. The flowers grow in a cluster of 5 to 15 on stems arising from the leaf axils. They are pea-shaped and erect with two broad upper petals, forming a semi-circle over the lower petals. The leaves are compound with a single pair of leaflets on a winged stalk and a branched tendril between them. Its fruit is a somewhat flattened pea pod. Sweet peas are poisonous when eaten-especially the flowers and the seeds.

201. Sweet Woodruff

- **Common name :** Wuderove, Wood-rova
- **Scientific name :** *Galium odoratum*
- **Family :** Rubiaceae
- **Native land :** Europe, Northern Africa, Northern Asia

Sweet woodruff is a flowering perennial plant. It has star-shaped fragrant leaves and small decorative white flowers. Bloom time is from April to June. It will spread naturally into an attractive mat of leaves and flowers. Flowers are small, fragrant (with four petals), white-coloured, which appear in loose cymes. Plants emit a strong odour of freshly mown hay when foliage is crushed or cut. Aromatic intensity of the foliage increases when dried; thus dried leaves are popularly used in sachets or potpourris. Plants have also been used commercially in perfumes. Leaves are sometimes used to flavour teas and cold fruit drinks.

202. Tamarack Larch

- **Common name** : American Larch/Black Larch/Hackmatack
- **Scientific name** : *Larix laricina*
- **Family** : Pinaceae
- **Native land** : Eastern North America

This plant is a small-to-medium-sized deciduous conifer. It is a forest tree of bogs/swamps. The tree has a straight, slender trunk and a narrow, open, pyramidal crown. The leaves are deciduous, needle-like. They are produced in clusters on short shoots or singly along the long shoots. They turn yellow during autumn and are shed in the same season. The fruits/cones are borne on short curving stalks. In its native place a decoction of the leaves has been used for diarrhoea and dysentery.

203. Taro

- **Common name** : Colocasia
- **Scientific name** : *Colocasia esculenta*
- **Family** : Araceae
- **Native land** : Wetlands of Malaysia

Taro is a herbaceous plant. It became a staple crop, cultivated for its large, starchy, spherical underground tubers, which are consumed as cooked vegetables. Young taro leaves are commonly used in the cooking of West and Central Africa. Taro corms (called taro roots) are short underground stems rich in starch. Unlike most starchy vegetables, they are high in amylose, a starch soluble in hot water, and contain 3% sugar which makes them somewhat sweet. Taro leaves and tubers are poisonous if eaten raw; the calcium oxalate they contain must first be destroyed by heating.

204. Thyme

- **Common name** : Garden Thyme
- **Scientific name** : *Thymus vulgaris*
- **Family** : Lamiaceae
- **Native land** : Southern Europe, the Mediterranean region, Asia Minor, and Central Asia

The plant is a small, low-growing shrub with curled branches. It is a perennial with a woody, fibrous root. There are three varieties usually grown for use, the broad-leaved, narrow-leaved and variegated. Thyme will grow on rocky soil and will spread over rocks and walkways. The plant has an agreeable aromatic smell and a warm pungent taste. The fragrance of its leaves is due to an essential oil, which gives it its flavouring value for culinary purposes. Thyme has various medicinal uses such as antiseptic, antispasmodic, tonic and carminative.

205. Tomatillo

- **Common name :** Husk Tomato, Mexican Husk Tomato
- **Scientific name :** *Physalis philadelphica*
- **Family :** Solanaceae
- **Native land :** Mexico

It is a small herb. All parts of the tomatillo plant are poisonous except the fruit, for which the plant is cultivated. This particular genus is characterised by the presence of pendant flowers and an envelope, known as the calyx or husk, which encloses the fruit. The tomatillo grows to an annual height of 1.2 metres. The fruit is large, round and sticky. The pulp of the tomatillo is a little sweeter than that of the tomato, and the flavour has been compared to an apple. The most common recipe for the tomatillo is salsa verde.

206. Tomato

- **Common name :** Tomato, Wolf Peach
- **Scientific name :** *Solanum lycopersicum*
- **Family :** Solanaceae
- **Native land :** South America

It is a short-lived perennial plant, grown as an annual plant. The plant has a weak woody stem that usually scrambles over other plants. The fruit is an edible, brightly coloured (usually red, from the pigment lycopene) berry. The fruit was believed to benefit the heart, as it contains lycopene, one of the most powerful natural antioxidants which, especially when cooked, has been found to help prevent various types of cancer. Tomatoes help to dissolve animal fat in butter, cheese, eggs, etc, preventing the hardening of the arteries, while the high potassium-content helps reduce high blood pressure.

207. Tree Tobacco

- **Common name :** Tree Tobacco, Mexican Tobacco
- **Scientific name :** *Nicotiana glauca*
- **Family :** Solanaceae
- **Native land :** North America

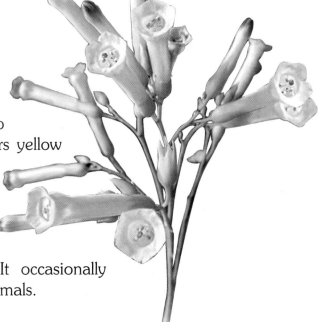

It is an evergreen perennial. The plant is an erect, slender, sparsely-branched perennial, soft-woody shrub to small tree, flowering throughout the year. The plant bears yellow flowers if given a long enough growing season. The 30-35 mm flower has a cylindrical corolla. Its leaves are attached to the stems by stalks and its leaves and stems are neither hairy nor sticky. The bloom time is spring and summer. All parts of the plants are highly poisonous and contain the toxic pyridine alkaloids nicotine and anabasine. It occasionally accumulates nicotine as a defence against herbivorous animals.

208. Tulip

- **Common name** : Tulip 'Barcelona'
- **Scientific name** : *Tulipa*
- **Family** : Liliaceae
- **Native land** : Eurasia from Austria and Italy eastward to Japan

It is a bulbous herb. The plants are generally found in a hilly country with extremely cold winters and hot dry summers. The stems are sturdy, making them ideal for windy or exposed spots, and the flowers are quite long-lasting. The tulip produces two or three thick, bluish green leaves that are clustered at the base of the plant. The usually solitary bell-shaped flowers have three petals and three sepals. Tulips are one of the most popular cut flowers across the world. The plants are harmful, if eaten, and may cause skin allergy.

209. Turnip

- **Common name** : Turnip
- **Scientific name** : *Brassica rapa subsp. rapa*
- **Family** : Brassicaceae
- **Native land** : Europe

It is a biennial that is grown as an annual. The plant can be harvested when mature or young. It can be cooked or eaten raw, and the young tops can be used like spring greens. Turnip leaves are usually light green, thin and sparsely pubescent (hairy). In addition, a white-fleshed, large global or tapered root develops at the base of the leaf petioles. The storage root varies in size but usually is 3 to 4 inches wide and 6 to 8 inches. The roots are a good addition to salads, pickles, or cooked in soups, stews, and side dishes.

210. Vine (Boston Ivy)

- **Common name** : Boston Ivy, Grape Ivy
- **Scientific name** : *Parthenocissus tricuspidata*
- **Family** : Vitaceae

Native land : China, Japan

Boston ivy is a rapid-growing, deciduous, woody perennial vine. It is a vigorous tendril climber that needs no support. It clings to surfaces (e.g., brick, stone or wood walls) by adhesive holdfasts (also called sucker discs) located at the tendril ends. Three-parted leaves are glossy dark green and are variable in shape. Greenish white flowers appear in late spring to early summer and give way to blue-black berries which are also hidden by the foliage and often not visible until autumn leaf-drop. Foliage turns scarlet red to scarlet purple in autumn. Foliage is semi-evergreen in warm climates.

211. Viola

- **Common name :** Heart's Ease Johnny Jump Up
- **Scientific name :** *Viola tricolor*
- **Family :** Violaceae
- **Native land :** Temperate Northern Hemisphere

Most violas are small perennial plants, but a few are annual plants and some are small shrubs. The flower, variable in colour, but not red, usually grows singly on a stalk and has five petals, four arranged in unlike pairs. The leaves may grow on the same stalk as the flower (stemmed violets) or on separate stalks (stemless violets). Violas are used as food plants by the larvae of some Lepidoptera species. Viola flowers are edible, used in medicines, as a laxative, and the flowers are candied for decoration in jellies, etc.

212. Warrigal Green

- **Common name :** Cook's Cabbage, New Zealand Spinach
- **Scientific name :** *Tetragonia tetragonioides*
- **Family :** Aizoaceae
- **Native land :** New Zealand, Australia, Japan, Chile and Argentina

It is a tender annual. The stems and the leaves of this spreading herb are covered with small, glistening, liquid-filled blisters. It is a sprawling plant with soft stems. It has light green leaves that are either triangular or arrow-shaped. Its small, yellow flowers appear from August to December. It is low in energy, has high water-content, is high in sodium and potassium. It was traditionally used as a food source, as a side for protein. It tastes like spinach and appropriate to incorporate into dishes as you would do so with spinach.

213. Water Fern

- **Common name :** Fishbone Water Fern, Forest Fern
- **Scientific name :** *Blechnum nudum*
- **Family :** Blechnaceae
- **Native land :** Australia

Fishbone water fern is a terrestrial, tufted fern of wet habitats. Blechnum species are commonly referred to as water ferns, as they are usually found in wet areas, growing in a variety of habitats from slopes to low-lying, poorly drained areas. It has a creeping horizontal underground stem (rhizome) which may form an erect sturdy trunk. It has bright-green fronds that are clustered near the tip of the rhizome. Each frond is supported by a stem (stipe). This kind of plant is mostly used in different gardening related works like sheltered gullies, beside water areas and ferneries.

214. Water Lettuce

- **Common name :** Water Lettuce
- **Scientific name :** *Pistia stratiotes*
- **Family :** Araceae
- **Native land :** Lake Victoria in Africa

Water lettuce is a free-floating, frost-tender aquatic perennial. It produces rosettes of wedge-shaped, overlapping, fluted, velvety, soft green leaves. The leaves are covered with water-repellant hair. The plant resembles the small open heads of lettuce. It is considered to be a noxious weed in many tropical and sub-tropical areas where it can quickly cover a pond or lake from shore to shore. Yellowish-green to creamy white flowers are generally inconspicuous. Feathery roots dangle downward from the plant, providing a shelter for many small fish. It is also sometimes commonly called shell flower. It is commonly used as an ornamental plant in water gardens.

215. Water Shield

- **Common name :** Water Shield, Dollar Bonnet, Fanwort
- **Scientific name :** *Brasenia schreberi*
- **Family :** Cabombaceae
- **Native land :** North America, California

Water shield is a small purple-flowered aquatic plant. It is found in northern ponds and still waters throughout the world, except in Europe. Each oval, floating leaf of water shield is 5-10 cm long. A long, jelly-coated stem connects the middle of the leaf to rootstocks buried in mud. Several leafstalks of varying lengths rise from the main stalk. The flowers are small and have three or four narrow petals; the small fruit is club-shaped. It is cultivated as a vegetable in China and Japan. It has some herbal properties as well.

216. Watercress

- **Common name :** Watercress
- **Scientific name :** *Nasturtium officinale*
- **Family :** Brassicaceae
- **Native land :** Europe and Asia

Watercress is an emergent perennial aquatic herb. Older leaves are compound with many wavy-edged, oval or lance-shaped leaflets growing from a central stalk. It has thin and fibrous roots at the bottom. The leaves taste very close to pepper. The plant blooms between March and October. The fruits are thin, slightly curved cylinders and contain four rows of small, round seeds. Watercress is commonly used as a salad green. It is also used as a garnish for meats and other dishes where a peppery or pungent flavour is desired.

217. White Bryony

- **Common name** : White Bryony, Wild Hop
- **Scientific name** : *Bryonia alba*
- **Family** : Cucurbitaceae
- **Native land** : Europe and Northern Iran

White bryony is a climbing perennial plant with vines. It can grow up to 50 feet tall. It has dark green, shiny leaves that resemble those of a cucumber plant (simple, five-lobed and petiolate, and rough to the touch). A single, unbranched tendril is associated with each leaf. Its yellowish white flowers, borne in small panicles, yield small green berries that turn dark purple in late summer. The root resembles a large white turnip. These large roots effectively fuel re-growth in spring. All parts contain bryonin which is poisonous and may cause illness or death.

218. Winter Cherry

- **Common name** : Ashwagandha, Winter Cherry, Indian Ginseng
- **Scientific name** : *Withania somnifera*
- **Family** : *Solanaceae*
- **Native land** : India, North Africa and the Middle East

Winter cherry is a short herbaceous perennial plant. It is an erect, many-branched shrub with very tiny green to yellow flowers. It grows well from hardwood cuttings which root quickly, or from seed. The branches are hairy that extend radially from a central stem. The flowers are small and green. The ripe fruit is orange-red. Ashwagandha is one of the most important herbs used in Ayurvedic medicine. The dried roots are the part used in Ayurveda medicines. It is renowned in India as the best rejuvenative herb.

219. Wisteria

- **Common name** : Chinese Wisteria
- **Scientific name** : *Wisteria sinensis*
- **Family** : Fabaceae
- **Native land** : China

Chinese wisteria is a deciduous perennial climbing vine. It grows up to 25 feet. It has racemes of mildly fragrant, pea-like, blue-violet flowers in May when the foliage is just beginning to expand. The flowers give way to pendant, velvety, bean-like seed pods which ripen in autumn and may persist into winter. The leaves are compound, odd-pinnate, and deep green. Over time, the stems of this vine become twisted, trunk-like and are massive. All parts of the plant contain a glycoside called 'wisterin' which is toxic, if ingested, and may cause nausea, vomiting, stomach pain and diarrhoea.

220. Yew

- **Common name :** Common Yew, European Yew
- **Scientific name :** *Taxus baccata*
- **Family :** Taxaceae
- **Native land :** Western, Central and Southern Europe, North-West Africa, Northern Iran and South-West Asia

Yew is the most popular evergreen tree. It is known as the 'tree of death'. The tree has spreading branches and slightly drooping branchlets. The bark is reddish brown and flaky, sometimes deeply fissured in very old trees. All parts of an English yew, except the fleshy aril surrounding the seed, contain alkaloids that are poisonous to humans and several other animals. Oil of yew is an intestinal irritant, responsible for colic and diarrhoea symptoms of yew poisoning. Today European yew is widely used in landscaping and ornamental horticulture.

221. Zinnia

- **Common name :** Zinnia, Youth-and-old-age
- **Scientific name :** *Zinnia elegans*
- **Family :** Asteraceae
- **Native land :** Mexico

Common zinnias are bushy, leafy annual plants. They have hairy, branching stems. The leaves of zinnia are arranged opposite to one another and they often clasp the stem. The solitary flower heads are borne at the ends of branches, growing at the junction of a leaflike structure and the receptacle. The flowers occur in a wide range of colours. The colours of the flower range from white and cream to pink, red, and purple, to green, yellow, apricot, orange, salmon and bronze. They make excellent fresh cut flowers.

Botanical Terms

1.	**Annual**	A plant that fully matures and produces seeds, and dies within one year.
2.	**Biennial**	A plant which completes its life cycle and dies within the second year.
3.	**Bloom**	To produce flowers
4.	**Cladode**	A shoot modified to assume the functions and usually the appearance of a leaf; often identifiable by arising in the axil of a modified leaf.
5.	**Corymb**	One in which the flower stalks arise at different levels on the main axis and reach about the same height and in which the outer flowers open first.
6.	**Deciduous**	A plant sheds its foliage at the end of the growing season.
7.	**Evergreen**	Evergreens are trees and shrubs that do not lose their leaves or needles at the end of their growing season. The leaves or needles stay the same colour throughout the year.
8.	**Foliage**	Leaf; the foliage leaves are probably the most noticeable parts of a flowering plant.
9.	**Herbaceous**	It is any non-woody plant, regardless of its flavour, scent or other properties. A herb cannot be a woody plant such as a tree or shrub.
10.	**Inflorescence**	Inflorescences are flower clusters.
11.	**Lanceolate**	Shape of a leaf; narrowly ovate and tapering to a point at the apex.

12.	Lyrate-pinnatifid	Shape of a leaf; leaf divided transversely into several lobes, the smallest at the base.
13.	Native	Indigenous origin or growth.
14.	Oblanceolate	Lanceolate with the narrow end at the base of the leaf.
15.	Ornamental	Decorative plant.
16.	Panicles	An inflorescence where the axis is divided into branches bearing several flowers.
17.	Perennial	Plants living for several years.
18.	Plume	A decoration made of feathers or something similar.
19.	Prairies	A large open grassland, especially in North America.
20.	Rhizomes	They are modified sub-terranean stem of a plant that is usually found underground, often sending out roots and shoots from its nodes. Rhizomes are also called creeping rootstalks and rootstocks.
21.	Succulent	Plants having thick fleshy leaves or stems adapted to storing water.
22.	Sucker	When a root sends up a new stem away from the main stem, it is called a sucker. Suckers are also any new vertical growth that arises from the base of a trunk.
23.	Trifoliate	A compound leaf having three leaflets.
24.	Tropical	Warm, hot, moist climate.
25.	Whorl	A whorl is a circle of the part of a flower that is present at a single level along the axis of a flower.